# Mothers Who Drive Their Daughters Crazy

## Ten Types of "Impossible" Moms and How to Deal with Them

Susan Simon Cohen
and Edward M. Cohen

Prima Publishing

PRIMA PUBLISHING and colophon are registered trademarks of Prima Communications, Inc.

**Library of Congress Cataloging-in-Publication Data**

Cohen, Susan (Susan Simon)
    Mothers who drive their daughters crazy: ten types of "impossible" moms and how to deal with them / Susan Cohen, Ed Cohen.
      p.  cm.
    ISBN 0-7615-0985-2
    1. Mothers and daughters.   2. Mothers—Psychology.
  I. Cohen, Edward M.  II. Title.
  HQ755.85.C625 1997
  306.874'3—dc21                                     97-19769
                                                      CIP

97 98 99 00 01 HH 10 9 8 7 6 5 4 3 2 1
Printed in the United States of America

---

**How to Order**

Single copies may be ordered from Prima Publishing, P.O. Box 1260BK, Rocklin, CA 95677; telephone (916) 632-4400. Quantity discounts are also available. On your letterhead, include information concerning the intended use of the books and the number of books you wish to purchase.

---

**Visit us online at www.primapublishing.com**

*For Blanche and Betty*

# Contents

# *Preface*

Susan and I have been married for nearly thirty years. Yet, on the surface, we seem a mismatched pair. Her career has taken a steady, clear, well-directed route. She knew in high school that she wanted to be a psychoanalyst, went to social work school immediately upon graduation from Brown, and gathered enough work experience to qualify for psychoanalytic training. She was accepted at the prestigious Postgraduate Center for Mental Health and has stayed connected to the Center throughout her career—as a supervisor, a training analyst, a teacher, assistant head of the Social Work Department, and now as director of the Introductory Program in Psychoanalytic Psychotherapy. At the same time, she has built a private practice.

My road has been bumpier. I started out as an actor, began to write, published stories and a novel that was optioned for Broadway. This returned me to the theater and I became part of the exciting off-off Broadway movement, writing plays, learning to direct, and running a small, nonprofit theater for many years. When I left that job, I returned to full-time writing, focusing on nonfiction.

It never occurred to us to work together until I was assigned an article on neurotic mothers by *Cosmopolitan* magazine. As I began researching this article, I found that when women start talking about their mothers, the emotion pours out, the words never stop, the relationship is described with difficulty and pain. I needed Susan to help me sort through the flood of feeling. We started talking, then listening to the interview tapes in the car, discussing what we had heard over breakfast, lunch, and dinner.

Before long, we knew we had a book, one that had to be written by the two of us. Mother–daughter relationships cannot be analyzed dryly. This is not a subject that can be illustrated with charts, statistics, and scholarly terms. It needed a writer who could re-create the intensity of the entanglement as well as one who could stand aside and see the patterns, point out universal trends, and define the stages of development that were, sometimes, being distorted.

So we started interviewing together; one woman recommended another. Everyone we approached agreed to talk, every daughter had stories to tell. We listened to college-aged women and middle-aged women and one woman in her sixties. We interviewed mothers and daughters, three generations of the same family, women who hated their mothers, and women who loved them. We read fictional portrayals of the relationship, autobiographies, professional books and journals, and consulted experts in the field.

What astonished us was the way women were discovering the fundamentals of the psychotherapeutic process on their own—learning to step aside and see what they were doing in a complex relationship, to connect the present to the past, to extricate themselves from powerlessness and take an active role in their lives—and how, once they did that, their behavior could change. We felt that it was important to write about this process the way they had learned it, not the way the textbooks spelled it out. This is, after all, a book about mothers and daughters, not about analysts and patients.

It has been a fascinating journey. We have learned a great deal, made friends, and come to a new appreciation of each other's talents—and of our own.

E. M. C.
New York City

# Acknowledgments

This book could not have been written without the contributions of the many women we interviewed. Their names have been changed to protect their privacy but they know who they are—and we thank them for their honesty, insights, and willingness to share their lives with us.

The mental-health professionals we interviewed are named in these pages and we are greatly indebted to them. We also wish to thank the following friends and colleagues who offered valuable advice and criticism: Janet Bachant, Ph.D.; Linda Cohen; William Finn; Sharon Messitte, C.S.W.; and Pauline Pinto, C.S.W. We are grateful to our agent, Noah Lukeman, for his support, to Irwin Cohen, Ph.D., for his computer know-how, and to the staff of the library at the Postgraduate Center for Mental Health. We owe a special debt to *Cosmopolitan* Senior Articles Editor Irene Copeland, who helped to get this project off the ground.

And, finally, thanks to our children and their mates, Noel and Donna, Joy and Neale, and our grandson, Emory, for the love and pleasure they bring to our lives.

# Introduction:
# Our Goals and Approach

When the actress Linda Lavin finished her stint as T.V.'s Alice, she was loved by millions of fans. She had made pots of money during the run of the series and there was more to come from syndication. She left with a network contract to produce and star in T.V. movies and headed back to New York, intent on making it on Broadway.

Lavin had worked hard to get where she was. She was proud of herself and had reason to be. She also knew what she wanted next and exactly how to get it. Hit-master Neil Simon had a new play, *Broadway Bound,* and the central character was based on Simon's mother. Lavin wanted that part. The character was fifty; Lavin was fifty. Simon said no. He thought she seemed too young for the role. Women of fifty in the 1930s, when the play was set, seemed older, he claimed, than women of fifty today. Lavin argued that Simon was remembering his own mother and that they always appear to us as older than they are. These two sophisticates shared a laugh over the powers our parents forever possess.

Lavin pleaded, kept phoning, wouldn't take no for an answer. Finally, she insisted that Simon allow her to audition—a rare concession for a star of her stature, but she knew what she was doing.

She had a period wig made up for the reading; she picked her clothes carefully. The woman who arrived at Simon's office was unrecognizable as the hip television star and she got the part. Not only that, but Simon was so bowled over by the way she played it that, during the first week of rehearsals, he wrote her a long monologue, which became the centerpiece of the play.

Lavin hit Broadway like a thunderstorm. Critics raved. Audiences loved her. The show was a sellout. Everybody said that she was a shoo-in for the Best Actress Tony, which, in fact, she eventually won. This woman at the peak of her career had the pleasure of knowing that she was there because she deserved it!

Then the day arrived when her mother came to see the show. Lavin is now a woman near sixty and her face still clouds over when she tells the tale. The performance went well, the audience gave her a standing ovation, she had heard her mother's laughter. Afterwards, Lavin's dressing room was mobbed. Yet what was the first thing Mom said as she entered, her voice rising above the hubbub?

"You gotta do something about that wig line! I'm sitting in the first row, nobody could have missed it!"

"No 'Nice show,' no 'Good job,' not even, 'Thank you for the lovely seats,'" says Lavin. She tries to laugh—then her eyes fill with tears and she looks like a deprived child. This is a painful reminder of how interaction with a mother can destroy all the achievement for which today's woman struggles so valiantly.

# Communication with Your Mother: What's Healthy, What's Not

Mothers and daughters throughout time have experienced crisscrossed communication and intense battles. In intimate connections, there are bound to be bumps. That does not make either party neurotic or evil or disturbed.

But when you are dealing with patterns of behavior with your mom that are constant and entrenched—patterns that were created in her childhood and have nothing to do with current reality—you are going to end up complaining that "she's driving me crazy!" You might label her interfering or troubled or irrational. Whatever the term, you are likely to feel frustration, fury, and, unfortunately, self-hatred.

The healthy mother initially creates a bond of safety and protection for her daughter and then, step by step, year by year, accomplishment by accomplishment, she lets her child go. She listens, she hears, she responds to you as you are— not to her wishes for you, not to her fantasies, not to her image of herself reflected in you. She treats you as the woman you are, not as the little girl you were, and you see her as the woman she is, not the woman you thought she was when you were a child.

In the relationship of two healthy adult women (who happen to be mother and daughter) both women are responding to who the other actually is. In the relationship of a mother and daughter who find themselves entrapped in perpetual tension, responses get swamped by fantasies, unexpressed feelings, and, more than anything else, deprivations from the past.

Because the mother–daughter relationship is so intense and important, it is often difficult for either party to figure out what exactly is going wrong when things go awry. Emotions tend to overwhelm intellect. The problems become paralyzing.

# Why We Developed the Personality Categories

In this book, we have tried to categorize difficult moms because, when dealing with tensions in life, the more specific you can be in defining the problem, the likelier you are to solve it. What was most upsetting to many of the women we met was that they felt overwhelmed and alone. The crises seemed to be chronic and the causes mysterious. The daughters were so burdened by pain and guilt that they could not step aside and see the patterns, identify what was happening, separate their feelings from their mothers', or differentiate her behavior from their reactions.

We listened to daughters and then grouped together similar stories, mapped out territories, and labeled each category. If you can spot your mother in one of these, you might be able to gain some objectivity, start seeing the patterns, and watch with a calmer eye. You will learn that you are not alone; you'll see that other daughters have similar experiences. You can then try to connect your mother's behavior with causes. You can learn to step out of the way of the darts, stop getting hurt, begin to take things less personally, and reduce the level of conflict.

# Learning to Accept Your Mother for Who She Is

"Dealing with my mother," says Elena, a twenty-six-year-old dancer, "is like dealing with someone from outer space. I'm trying to communicate real, current information. She's hearing voices from the past. Why am I knocking my head against the wall? What she's responding to has nothing to do with the present, nothing to do with reality. She is locked into patterns that are not going to change—certainly I am not going to change them. For whatever reason, she is never going to approve of herself, of me, of my husband, or of anything else in my life. I don't know why this is but I'll tell you one thing I know for sure: *It's not my fault!"*

With these words, Elena was headed toward freedom. She was not happy to see her mother trapped in this way. Elena would have liked to have had a mother who could experience pleasure in her daughter's achievements. Unfortunately, given her mother's personality traits, this is unlikely to happen. However, because Elena was able to step aside and identify the patterns, she was, at least, free of the responsibility and guilt for her mother's behavior.

Florence Miller Radin, a psychotherapist in San Mateo, California, says, "Adult children who keep trying to 'make it' with inadequate, unloved, and unloving parents are like people who go to a vegetarian restaurant and demand roast beef. The parents on whom they make demands for enlightened parenting never got it from their own parents. They do not have it in stock and they are not able to provide it for their children."

Once you have acknowledged this in your relationship with your mother, there is some relief. Seeing her as she is, seeing her whole, seeing what you like about her and what you don't, seeing what you can deal with and what you can't, seeing her as human and troubled instead of omnipotent—these are giant steps toward health and peace. They reduce her power over your life, allow you to take responsibility for your own behavior, set limits on the amount of pain she can cause, and help you to distinguish the present from the past.

As you begin to change your expectations of what she can and cannot offer, perhaps you'll learn to shrug off her

shortcomings with a smile. Most important, you can maintain the relationship, learning to take the bad along with the
good so that you do not have to discard the parts about her
that you like in yourself.

# Clarifying the Mother-Daughter Relationship

Once we had grouped mothers by the types of stories their
daughters told, by the similarity in their traits, and once we
had labeled the groups according to behavior, we further
clarified our work by breaking it down into several points.

1. In each chapter, we look at good relationships as well as
   poor ones. We believe that the impulse in every child is
   toward growth and independence. Watch any infant
   struggling to take that next step—to lift her head in the
   crib, to crawl, to walk, to talk—and you can't help but
   marvel at the human's innate desire to move in the right
   direction. It is important to look at such natural development in order to understand why and where it goes
   wrong.
2. Although we tried to differentiate each type of mother,
   the categories overlap. There are moms we call Critics
   who also have elements of Controllers. Often, they are
   Competitors, too. An intrusive mother can shift and slide
   and dizzy you with her changing tactics. That is one of
   the reasons that trying to define her can be frustrating.
3. Most mothers are neither totally disturbed nor paragons
   of mental health. Even healthy moms have anxieties.
   "Good enough" moms go through bad periods. Loving
   people make mistakes. By identifying your mom and by
   comparing her to other moms, you are better equipped
   to spot the dangerous currents and suspect signals and
   separate them from her good qualities.

4. There are some terrific mothers of infants who are not so terrific when the child becomes a toddler. There are some mothers who are great when it comes to offering affection but have no grasp on handling hostility. Some mothers fall apart when their daughter hits puberty. Some become overly possessive just when their child is ready to leave the nest. Moms can be positive role models in one stage of life and totally inept in another.

5. Throughout the book, we have traced the arc of female development from infancy to adulthood, investigating some of the areas where difficulties are likely to occur with different types of mothers. The chapter subtitles highlight this thread, and by following it, we hope you will gain some understanding of your own needs and how they were—or were not—met. By seeing the various facets of your mother as she reacted to you at different times (sometimes positively and sometimes negatively) and by understanding how seeds that were planted early on blossomed (to the good or the ill), you should be able to see your current relationship with your mother more clearly. Learning about your needs at individual stages in life will help you to get a picture of what past deprivations you might be clinging to in your relationship today.

## Changing Your Relationship with Your Mother

Although figuring things out requires a lot of delving into memory, the primary question is, What can you do about it now? We believe that you *can* change your relationship with your mother and that you *must* change your relationship with the people you are using to stand in for her.

This book is addressed to adult daughters who remain enmeshed with their mothers, repeating old patterns that prevent them from moving into a stage of life where they are free to make their own choices. It is basically concerned with your relationship with Mom in adulthood: how a dysfunctional relationship limits your options, how it undermines your other relationships.

Handling the difficult mother takes more than learning some pat phrases for "better communication." The trouble with such advice is that you memorize the phrases but Mom changes the topic and once again you are at a loss to regain control. Our approach is not to try to outmanipulate her. Rather, it is to help you to understand Mom in order to understand yourself and find some freedom from the past so as to be able to live fully in the present with your lover, boyfriend, husband, friend, or daughter.

In the end, our approach follows the fundamentals of problem-solving in every relationship, and any advice we have to offer about one particular type of mother may apply just as well to all:

1. Recognize that there is a problem and acknowledge how you feel about it.
2. Separate the present from the past so that you can define what the conflict is about.
3. Acknowledge what you are contributing to the situation.
4. Face what you are gaining from the entanglement and the loss you will feel when you resolve it.
5. Deal with the anxiety you will experience from making a change.
6. Translate your insights into action by taking one step at a time and allowing each small step to lead to a larger one.

Once you have conquered these techniques, you are on your way to better interactions with your mother as well as your father, siblings, friends, spouse, and children.

Still, there is no underrating problems with your mom because of the amount of power she has had in your life.

This is the woman who comforted you when you cried as an infant, who offered food when you were hungry, who induced sleep when you were tired, who reassured when you were frightened. To differentiate who she is now from that overpowering presence is one of the most difficult steps in resolving the issues between you.

Reading this book in order to point your finger and cry, "Look what you did to me!" will not solve the problem. If she is doing it to you still, if you are doing to others what she once did to you, if you are finding others to do now what she did then, some serious self-searching is required. You may not have created the pattern, but if you are invested in maintaining it for your own reasons, the interaction becomes extremely harmful to both mother and daughter as well as to everyone else in their lives.

## Separation and Strategies for Change

What's the ultimate goal? It is the freedom to be yourself and to make your own choices. This is achieved through *separation,* a developmental process that establishes your psychological, physical, and emotional individuality. Separation allows you to reduce your mother's impact. You learn to differentiate your identity from hers, to distinguish your desires from hers, and to take control of your life.

A mother may have a strong desire to see her infant as a cuddly doll, but the baby immediately interacts like a separate person. The baby seeks to engage the mother, responds to her stimulation, and is aware of her responses. Gradually, the child learns to define her body as separate from the rest of the world—an amazing bit of comprehension—and she learns that her desires may also be different. Separation is an arduous and complex task, which starts virtually at birth and takes place in gradual steps over a lifetime.

However, the process can be stalled and daughters often have to restart the engine in adulthood. It is this phenomenon that we will be investigating—the efforts of grown daughters to separate after a lifetime of entanglement. They do this by learning about their own needs, by getting in touch with their inner voice, and by setting boundaries on the intrusions of the outside world.

In each chapter, we propose some strategies that will help you to change the way you relate to your mother and to people like her and to see that all good and all bad does not flow from her, that her praise or criticism does not make or break your achievement, and that your life is your own—not hers. Of primary importance is creating relationships that exist without her shadow hovering, for when it does it forces you to behave in ways that only serve to maintain your connection to her.

Separation and the accompanying personal changes are not minor accomplishments. When you consider that you can manage these changes without Mom making any significant ones herself, your win becomes even more of a triumph. That triumph, when it comes, will be a smile or a shrug when she behaves as she always has, a sense of freedom when her criticism rolls right off your back. You might not be able to tell her what you have won; she might not be happy if she knew.

Still, you will be filled with warmth and pride where there used to be rage and self-hatred. You will feel that an impossible burden has finally been lifted off your back, allowing you to walk into the future with a lighter, happier step.

# 1

# The Narcissist

## *The Infant's Need for Mirroring*

**W**hen Wendy, thirty-five, made partner—the youngest in her law firm—she and her husband, Andy, went out for dinner and ordered champagne. He toasted her. She couldn't stop beaming. Then Wendy spoke the dreaded words:

> "I'd like to drive up to Connecticut to tell Mom and Dad this weekend. You know, instead of over the phone. It would be so nice to see their faces!"
>
> Andy nodded reluctantly, knowing all too well what was going to happen.
>
> It had been clear from their first hello that Wendy's mom thought that nothing would ever be good enough for her beloved daughter. Mom hadn't approved of their

wedding plans. She hadn't liked the dress Wendy had chosen. The neighborhood of their first apartment hadn't been fashionable enough for her. Every vacation they had ever taken was to a spot she had visited and disliked. Wendy kept saying that her mother behaved like this because she loved her so much.

"This is love?" Andy would moan.

Every time Wendy said, "Let's go visit Mom and Dad this weekend," Andy knew what it meant. Wendy would put on a brand-new outfit and Mom would respond by saying she looked too skinny or too fat. Dad was sweet and meant well, but it was Mom Wendy wished to see, usually with some tiny bid for approval—a funny story about an old friend or something nice that had happened at work.

Andy says, "My heart would be trembling as Wendy, seated beside me in the car, smiled in anticipation of Mom's pleasure because her response was always the same. In some subtle, icy way, Mom would fail to approve and Wendy would pretend that she hadn't expected otherwise."

At first on that particular visit, it looked like everything was going well. They were in her parents' living room, nibbling on cheese and crackers, when Wendy, smiling shyly, said, "I've got something to tell you, Mom and Dad. I've been promoted to partner."

Both parents glanced at one another and then looked at their daughter with pride. Andy breathed a little easier. Wendy felt tears of joy beginning to simmer. There was a moment of satisfied silence, as if everyone was so happy that no words would do. Then, her mother announced, "Well, first thing I'll do is take you shopping because you can't go to the office any more looking like that!"

Of course, she laughed her little-girl laugh as though she had just said the nicest thing in the world and her adoring husband laughed along. Andy's jaw dropped as he waited for Wendy to tell her mother to go to hell. But Wendy, her smile quivering, murmured that this ugly suit was just something she had thrown on without thinking anyway.

By the time they had gotten into their car for the drive home, Wendy was convinced that her mother was only concerned for her daughter's success. After all, Mom was right. Wendy had to change her image now, when it was crucial that she looked good and svelte—like Mom did. It was wonderful, according to Wendy, to have a mother who was such a gorgeous and admirable role model.

"And don't forget 'loving,'" sneered Andy, which he knew at once he shouldn't have said because he instantly became the bad guy. They ended up fighting and, when they got home, Wendy sank into a funk, sitting up all night and bingeing on cheesecake.

## Qualities of the Narcissist

The most significant quality of the Narcissist—and the most damaging—is that she is oblivious to her impact on you because she is so involved in admiring herself. Wendy's mother treats her daughter as an extension of herself, there only to take care of her needs; she is unaware of her daughter as a separate person with feelings of her own. Rather than recognizing that she has wiped Wendy's achievement off the map by criticizing her clothing, she sees herself as giving and protective—and insists that she be loved and admired for her generous behavior!

If you have been brought up by this kind of mother, you may feel like you are in a maze. Everyone tells you how wonderful and gorgeous and compassionate she is when all you sense are the constant put-downs. The Narcissist always seems to be in the right, always seems to do things so well that you end up not trusting your gut responses. Instead of feeling attacked by her and deeply hurt, you twist yourself into knots of guilt. You take it out on your husband, you take it out on your kids, and of course, you take it out on yourself. The Narcissist's destructive influence rules your life and you can't even get mad at her!

"My mother gave me a vase when I moved into a new apartment," says Stephanie, twenty-four. "I changed its place. When my mother came to visit, the first thing she said was, 'You moved my vase. I liked it better over there!'

"How do you respond to that?" asks Stephanie. "My first thought was, Did she really say that? Did it mean what it sounded like? If I object, she's going to accuse me of nit-picking and we're going to have one of our constant fights and, after she leaves, one of my aunts is going to call and tell me that I'm an ungrateful kid and that my mother is crushed, and all because she was loving and generous enough to give me a beautiful, tasteful gift. And, of course, my aunt will know where it came from—a fine store, to be sure. And, of course, it cost a fortune and here I am, accusing her of heaven-knows-what instead of listening to her advice on interior design and, would you believe, when I get off

the phone I truly do not know whether I am nuts or
not, but every time I look at the damned vase I burst
into tears!"

The Narcissist has a double-barrel in her arsenal because
not only is she self-involved and unresponsive to your
needs, she also has taught you since birth that only *her*
needs are important and that, if you fail to fulfill them, you
have committed the worst sin a daughter can perpetrate.

Can you imagine having a more narcissistic mother than
Marlene Dietrich? In her biography of her mother (*Marlene
Dietrich,* Knopf, 1993), Maria Riva paints a devastating picture of a woman who was always playing roles, always performing for the applause of others. Dietrich approached
motherhood as another terrific role. Suddenly she was to be
called "Mutti" by her husband, relatives, and friends. Everyone had to admire her loving concern for her newborn.
Dietrich insisted on breastfeeding her baby but, for the rest
of her daughter's life, Maria was made to feel guilty because
her mother had sacrificed her youthful breasts to her daughter's greed!

## The Healthy Mother and the Infant

Nothing is more fascinating to a newborn than her mother.
She communicates with her hands, her voice, her body. Her
smell becomes familiar and comforting. Her eyes glisten.
Her teeth appear and disappear. Her nose wiggles. Mom
laughs, coos, sings. She beams with love.

The healthy mother is delighted when we make our
own sounds. She encourages us to try new things and she
brings the world to us. She communicates, she hears, she
listens, she responds. She mirrors.

The act of mirroring is how we make our first definitions of ourselves. Mother tells us and shows us that we will be loved, unconditionally and forever, just because we are lying there in her arms, performing acts we didn't even know we knew how to do. Everything we do, she celebrates as a magnificent achievement. We are the center of her attention, her concern and her delight. This is a lesson that never leaves us.

The healthy mother assures us that we can make known our wants and needs, we can achieve satisfaction, we can assert power. She colors her words with tones that the child learns to read as easily as she learns the meaning of the words. By reflecting, by responding, by enjoying, by encouraging, Mom helps us learn how to communicate and that what we are saying and feeling is important. This act of mirroring is the bedrock on which our sense of self is based. If our feelings have been enjoyed and responded to from the beginning, we will learn to trust them.

## The Narcissist and the Infant

The narcissistic mother comes to her newborn with unsatisfied yearnings of her own. She is or has been unloved. Perhaps she is in a bad marriage and is unfulfilled as a person. She may be frightened and have little identity or self-esteem. She sees the infant as someone to fill these gaps, not as a wonderful new creature who is going to learn and grow. The baby's total dependency gives the Narcissist a sense of purpose and power she has never before achieved. Being a mother means that she is finally admired, adored, constantly watched, as if her responses and needs were the most important things in the world. If she was not adequately mothered as an infant herself, she is, in fact, experiencing these sensations for the very first time—only the positions have been reversed.

A mother who uses her child to mirror her instead of being the one doing the mirroring is a narcissistic mother. The problem arises when the sweet little baby starts crying and won't stop. Mother gets angry. Why? Because the baby is not making her happy! The Narcissist wants a doll to hold and cuddle. She doesn't want a toddler who will explore and make a mess. She doesn't want a teenager with developing ideas of her own.

The mother's unfulfilled needs are the focus of this distorted relationship and become the very air the infant breathes. Most likely, when the daughter has a daughter, she will pass on the role reversal.

## What's Behind Mom's Behavior?

Marlene Dietrich's mother had a very rough life. She was pushed into marriage as a young girl with a notorious rake, whom the family wanted to marry off before he got caught in a scandal. After his death left her alone with two infant daughters, she wore mourning black at her second wedding to an older man who offered security. Her first set of in-laws called her "that poor child"; the second set refused to have anything to do with her because she was of a lower class.

Is it any wonder that this deprived woman turned to her daughter to fulfill all her longings? Is it any wonder that pretty, wily, strong-willed Dietrich learned that she would have to find ways to fill her needs elsewhere? This she did by sculpting her body into a work of art, by surrounding herself with adoring sycophants, by turning her daughter into yet another servile flatterer.

This behavior of the child of an ungiving mother can be seen as an act of survival, of strength. By developing into a Narcissist, by demanding that the world supply her with what she had been deprived of as a child, Marlene was saving herself. When she gave birth to her daughter, Dietrich supplied her damaged self with the mother she had never had.

Once the pattern is set, it is difficult to change. As the years pass, it is always the mother's needs that overwhelm the household. Her crises, her fears, her moods get all the attention. It is not necessary for this kind of mom to be a glamorous movie star. She can be a sickly woman who needs constant tending or a workaholic corporate executive. She can be depressed and withdraw into her room for days except when she needs to unburden herself. And who better to dump on than her daughter?

"My parents' marriage was awful," says Amy, thirty. "My father groveled for my mother's love. He didn't get it but she agreed to stay with him for the sake of the kids. Even when I was little, she would pour out her heart to me and say that if it weren't for me, she wouldn't know what to do. I was her strength."

This kind of a relationship between mother and daughter can be intense, dramatic, entangled, and, to the daughter, attractive. Feeling so needed and grown up can be seductive.

"The bargain was," says Amy, "if I stayed close, if I listened to her, calmed her, always did as she said, she would love me always and we would always have these heart-to-hearts across the kitchen table, hands clutched tightly. I wanted her love more than anything so, of course, I complied."

It took many years for Amy to realize that she wasn't being loved, she was being used.

"My mother was the one who ran the show," says Amy now. "She was the Queen Bee and I was her marionette."

## What's in Store for the Narcissist's Daughter?

The truly loving mother offers us her love simply because we are, not because of how we perform. This stable, sheltering nurturing gives us a sense of value on which all else can be built. It can never be taken away, no matter what mistakes or failures lie ahead.

The daughter of a Narcissist, however, expresses only what she has learned will get her love and approval.

Dietrich's daughter, Maria Riva, lived in an entirely artificial environment for a child, yet she adjusted to formal dinners, being surrounded by adults, speaking only when spoken to and then only what her mother wished to hear. This little girl developed impeccable manners, learned to handle an array of silverware and five different-sized wine glasses. She sat with a rigid spine at the table, smiling politely and keeping her eye on her glamorous mom, eating when she began eating, using the utensil she used, and never knowing that she was being cheated out of a childhood.

This daughter becomes totally dependent on her mother because she has not developed a sense of herself. The less secure and lovable she feels, the more she turns to her mother instead of herself, seeing Mom as beautiful, wise, and, heaven help us, loving.

Andrea, in her late twenties, sits on the edge of her chair, tailored, chic, removing lint from her skirt. She is smart and outspoken, quick to criticize, and she discusses her past as if she were talking about a third person:

"I felt like I was a doll to my mother, not real, something you could put down when you were finished. All her love for me was directed at the outside world. She was forever telling people how wonderful I was, but there was never any stroking, fondling, kissing for me. I always felt that she was saying 'Look what I produced!' You'd think I would have been angry, yet, the first time I was away from her, when I went off to college, I felt like I was in a horrible void, like I was deep-sea diving and the oxygen had been cut off. I never drank in high school and started in college and that was a major deal because my mom doesn't drink at all. She assumed that I was drinking because I gained a lot of weight but, even without that, she just knew. My mom knows everything about me. If I don't tell her, she knows anyway."

The Narcissist's daughter has been brought up feeling that being loved depends on her performance and, even more so, on external reaction. It is only Mother's approval that gives her value and that has to be struggled for, over and over again, because children who are burdened with the task of fulfilling a parent's fantasies are certain to disappoint. The daughter has no way of interpreting her mother's turning away other than as a response to some mysterious bad thing she has done or, even worse, as a response to the bad thing she is.

Instead of saying that Mom is hateful, the Narcissist's daughter turns her anger against herself and says, "I am hateful."

As one daughter described it:

"You are in a situation where you need your mother's love because you have never been given it unconditionally; you can't get angry with her because the love she offers has been so tenuous that you are terrified of losing it; and you can't ever win the kind of love you need because of her own limitations. You are in a bind that is dizzying, you can't see your way out, you have learned a way of relating that is going to poison the rest of your life, and you feel it is all your fault."

These women, as adults, suffer from feelings of emptiness, of always being unsatisfied, of having flaws; yet they feel guilty and foolish because they cannot put their finger on why they are suffering. They fall into codependency in relationships, depressions, melancholia. They try to fill the gap with too much eating, too much shopping, too many men—but nothing does the trick until they face what it is they are actually missing.

### Three Generations: The Legacy of a Narcissist

Nina, now a woman in her late thirties, never knew her grandmother, Rebecca, but Claire, Nina's mom, kept the legend alive. Rebecca was a powerhouse; a college graduate in the 1920s, when that was an astonishing feat for a woman. An early suffragette, she made headlines as the first woman to hitchhike across America unchaperoned—a daredevil feat to demonstrate women's courage and determination.

But Rebecca had failed to pass on these qualities to her daughter. Although Claire was multitalented and ambitious, her tales of her mother's achievements were always tinged with the sad awareness of her own lacks.

Claire left college to run away with an older man, Dean, who at the time was flush with money, dashing, and handsome; he wore a ruby pinkie ring, which turned Rebecca against him for life. When Claire told the story about the pinkie ring, Nina sensed that there was a nasty, contemptuous side of Rebecca that was never really discussed.

Claire and Dean moved to California—as far away from her mother as Claire could get. She wrapped her life around Dean's desire to impress the movers and shakers, producing two children, Paul and Nina, but she quickly found the truth in the maxim that those who marry young marry their mothers. Life with Dean was no different from life with Rebecca. It was all about his dreams of success, his conquests, his needs. She and the children were merely props in the picture. Nina was once again serving, in awe of someone she depended upon, only this time she had picked someone who didn't deserve it. When the money ran out, Dean turned on his wife with a vengeance.

Claire returned East with the two toddlers and, although it would have been simple to crawl back to her mother's home and eat humble pie ("You were right, Ma. I'll never do it again. I'll always listen to you in the future."), Claire resisted. She set up a life of her own and found a way to support herself and her kids as a reporter and then an editor. Nina still remembers when her mother filled her with pride, when she was raring to go each day, doing work that she liked, pleased with her achievements, and winning recognition in her field.

But somehow it wasn't enough. After all, what could top Rebecca's hitchhiking across America? Claire entered a period when she came home from work suffering migraines, depressed and exhausted. She retreated each night to her bed and began using liquor and pills to ease the pain. Nina watched in agony as her mother fell apart. She felt that it was up to her to cheer Claire up and ease her pain. Her brother, Paul, on the other hand, rebelled against the bleakness of the house. He resolved his discomfort by getting away—to the streets, to his friends, to other families. Claire took out much of her anxiety and frustration on him; mother and son fought constantly for control.

Nina played the role of peacemaker. She pleaded with Claire to go easier on Paul, then she pleaded with Paul to accommodate Claire. She passed messages from one to the other, often prettying up the wording. She was alert to any sign of tension and felt that it was up to her to head off the explosions. She turned herself into a responder, a negotiator; always attuned to others' needs, she never trusted that her needs were important or that anyone would pay attention to them.

In a remarkable demonstration of how children can turn problems into assets, how they strive for healthy resolutions of the most destructive situations, Nina fell into a career that seemed like a natural for her. In high school, she worked as a receptionist for a talent agent, and it was a field she knew that she could conquer. She studied law and business in college, but what she had intuitively was the ability to handle high-strung artists, because she knew how to accept herself as a background character, to appease, to calm, to be a stand-in.

Although it was a way of denying everything raging within her, professionally, it worked. The more she kept her feelings at bay, the more adept she became at negotiations. She became a top agent with a reputation for taking care of her clients, winning them the best deals, and never getting ruffled.

Despite her success, Nina found herself to be unhappy, frightened, anxious. "I had molded my life, created myself, developed my talents, all to fit everyone else's needs," she says. "Where was I in this picture?"

Claire, on the other hand, was delighted. The money was rolling in. Some of the glamour of her daughter's career rubbed off on her. Renewed and replenished by Nina's success, Claire found a new life by marrying a wealthy attorney, Bert, who installed her in a beautiful suburban home. Nina says now, "She was his showpiece. I was hers."

Claire leapt into her role as wife and elegant hostess. Bert was delighted. So was Nina. "It shows how little we know about the people we love. Here I was suffering because I was living only for the approval of others, especially her. Yet I thought it was wonderful and glamorous and totally right that she perform so well on Bert's behalf. I remember she used to prepare an exquisite salmon mousse for her parties, and for the center she would peel a tomato—imagine, peeling a tomato all in one unbroken ribbon—and she would curl the skin to form a rosebud. She would never allow any of the kitchen help to do it, this was her work of art and I used to think it was a magnificent achievement. With all my success, I could never peel a tomato! What is astonishing is that we were both desperate to satisfy our needs, yet neither had an inkling of how to go about it.

"Everything was muffled in those years. I was close to her, full of admiration, completely under her thumb, unaware of how unhappy I was. Until I married Charlie. That tore the picture apart."

True to the family tradition, Nina picked a man much like her mother: self-absorbed, needy, dramatic, glamorous. He was a painter and his life overwhelmed hers. Despite the fact that she was their prime financial support, it was his work that was always talked about, his life that was always in the spotlight. Claire detested him at first glance.

"Maybe if she hadn't been so opposed I wouldn't have married him," says Nina. "But I had to get away from her and thought this was the way to do it. Little did I realize that I was replacing her with another Narcissist."

The years turned difficult. Charlie hated Claire as much as she hated him. Nina felt obliged to play mediator again, just as she had between her brother and her mother. "It seemed," says Nina, "that we had not moved one inch as a family in thirty years."

The situation exploded over dinner one night when Charlie was moaning about his career problems. Claire airily dismissed him by saying, "Oh Charlie, as far as I'm concerned, you don't have a career!"

"She thought she was making a joke," says Nina, "but poor Charlie, who, for all his faults, worked like a demon and had a great deal invested in his art, was crushed. I stared across the table as though I had never seen my mother before.

"It was the total dismissal of another human being—her obliviousness to the fact that he would be hurt—that shocked me. She obliterated him, albeit with a laugh and charm, just the way Rebecca must have done to Dean because of his ruby pinkie ring."

This is the most significant and destructive sign of the Narcissist; they are so focused on their own thwarted needs that they can't imagine you will be disturbed when they step all over yours.

"My mother had done this to me all my life and I had never acknowledged it," says Nina, "but when she did it to Charlie, that was my turning point."

Nina pulled away from Claire altogether: didn't see her, didn't talk to her, and tried to reshape her life around her marriage. It did not work because Charlie began to self-destruct. He became an alcoholic and stopped painting; his needs overwhelmed the relationship so that Nina was finally able to see that she had simply substituted one Narcissist for another. If she was going to figure things out, she realized, escaping from Claire was not enough. She had to escape from all the Claire substitutes as well.

"Once I had left Charlie," she says, "I could see that Claire had been right about him. Narcissistic mothers are often brilliant women and, if they aren't, you think that they are. They are often gorgeous. They are slender when you are chubby. And they are certainly adept at spotting competing Narcissists. But these are not necessarily the qualifications for being a good mother. The problem is that all this is impossible to see when you are the daughter. It wasn't until I was on the outside and could recognize how destructive her behavior was to

Charlie that I knew I had to escape from her dangerous influence over my life."

## Separation: The First Step

New York City psychotherapist Roberta Schultz says, "There is no way to get through to a narcissistic mother because her mother was probably even more disturbed, and the only way she could adapt was to turn off to anyone else's needs and pay attention to her own. Therefore, the pattern began as a way of protecting herself in childhood, and the daughter is fighting a losing battle, hoping to change it. However, once the daughter sees this—even though she'll never like it—perhaps she can accept the mother's behavior."

One of the ways to learn to accept your mother's behavior is to separate yourself from it so that it does not rule your life. The most difficult and painful step in the separation process is the first one—that moment of standing aside and taking a good look at what is going on. Once you take that step, you're well on your way to breaking out of the vicious cycle.

When you are caught in the cycle, you tend to be blinded by it. You want to maintain the security of what you have always known so you repeat the pattern in relationship after relationship. However, in order to change your life and find a more satisfying route, the first thing you must do is to take a good look and see!

For Maria Riva, Dietrich's daughter, at twenty already an alcoholic and a divorcée, the moment occurred when she read a book, *The Neurotic Personality of Our Time,* by psychoanalyst Karen Horney. Riva was startled to find her innermost wounds being exposed and explained by a total stranger, without censure. She realized that if her desperation and self-hatred could be written about, that there must be others like her.

Sometimes, that first moment of "seeing" does not come out of a book or interaction with your mother, but out of something that happens in another relationship. Somehow, you are jolted out of acceptance and begin to trace the pattern back to your relationship with Mom. That's okay, so long as you begin to recognize the pattern at work—that your needs are not being met—and you stop thinking "something is wrong with me!"

Mia, twenty-three, was a graduate student at a large Midwestern university, working on her Ph.D. dissertation. She had set aside the summer for research and preparing for her orals while her lover, Ethan, traveled around Europe.

Three weeks after he left, she received an emergency phone call from Ethan. He had to see her. He had something urgent to tell her. Nothing was so important that she could not put it aside and spend a week with him. She tried to explain that she had a schedule of appointments and interviews set up. Taking a week out at this short notice would put her behind and harm her reputation with her advisers and the department. Nevertheless, he insisted that she fly out to hear what he had to say. There was no one else in the world that he could talk to about this. It was absolutely imperative!

As usual, Mia did what Ethan demanded. Her first night there, he announced that their relationship was over, that he had met someone else and was madly in love. But it was important to him that Mia meet his new love, he wanted her approval, he wanted to know that they could still be friends!

"What astonished me," says Mia, "was that it had never occurred to him that I would be hurt or angry. He was so tied up in his needs that he had assumed that I would be happy—simply because his needs had been met. I had never seen the similarity between Ethan and my mother before but there it was. She had never acknowledged that I had existed as separate from her, either. She, too, never knew when she was hurting me. She was oblivious to my needs, to my reactions, to my existence. That's being erased as a person. That's being told you don't exist. Or that you exist only as someone else's mirror. And if you're told that often enough you'll believe it.

"I grabbed the first flight home. I was so shocked I couldn't even explain it to Ethan and, for the first time in my life, didn't give a damn whether he understood or not. But a couple of things were clear that had never been clear before: One, that this was not my fault; two, that I would have to make major changes in my life; and, three, that my mother was not the person to call to discuss them!"

When our needs have not been met in infancy, when something has gone wrong, when roles have been reversed, we can spend our entire lives trying to right the wrongs—in our love lives, at work, and in our concepts of ourselves. We are attracted to people who fit into our memories, we manipulate them into playing roles we need filled, we re-enact ancient scenes trying to find satisfaction and relief— yet as long as we repeat the cycle we never do.

We keep repeating the original cycle for many powerful reasons: because it is all we know, because it punishes us for what we erroneously felt was our fault, because it provides us with profound connections to people who were desperately needed, because it reminds us of when we felt safe, because we figure maybe this time it will work out.

# Strategies for Change

- Avoid knocking heads. A head-on confrontation with a Narcissist is not going to pay off. She is not going to change; her pattern is too deeply established, her needs are too embedded. You might, with excruciating patience, get her to change some behavior. You might get her to be a little nicer to you. But as to changing her feelings or her fears, forget it. She will forever want to be the Queen of the Manor, with you as her lady-in-waiting.
- Return to the source. The only way to straighten out the past is to go back to the source, see it the way it was, and change your relationship to it. You can do this by seeking the help of a third eye—a book, a friend, a sister, a therapist—who will help you to see things more clearly.
- Talk about your feelings! Talking brings up new thoughts, surprises, buried memories. Out of the collage, you begin to piece together the real picture. The more you talk about your feelings, the more you will be able to connect them with childhood causes and the less your present will be burdened with the past. Articulating the problem is a help in itself. You find a way out of the maze, begin to differentiate cause and effect, and objectively look at what is going on. Confirmation of what you see and feel can be greatly freeing. It allows you to give up denial and self-doubt, permits you to accept your anger when justified, confirms your ability to assess and evaluate, and, most importantly, allows you to let go and move on.

# 2

# The Controller
## *The Toddler Struggles for Autonomy*

*T*he period of intense mother–infant bonding does not last forever. Mom may want her baby to stay nestled in her arms but you, without even knowing the eventual goal, struggle to turn over, to move, to achieve some form of autonomy. This impulse is as natural as breathing. It is, at the start, undefeatable and—if your mother is a Controller—it means big trouble.

> Francesca, forty-two, says, "People beam when they tell me how wonderful my mom was. How she would sit me in her lap for hours—*hours!*—and brush my hair. My every outfit was perfect and color-coordinated. She crocheted blankets for me and made my clothes and changed my dainty shirts if there was a single stain.

I don't remember any of this but I cringe for the poor child I was, forced to sit there and get her hair brushed, unable to make a move without Mom complaining about a crease in her dress. It took me years to start battling her, but when I did, I made up for all those brushing sessions but good!"

# Qualities of the Controller

From your earliest infancy, the Controller burdens your life and daily existence with unwritten rules and codes of behavior—many of which make sense to no one but herself. She doesn't explain to you why the dos and don'ts exist—thereby teaching you how decisions and codes are arrived at, enabling you to make up your own mind when faced with a new situation. Rather, the Controller's commands issue directly from some unseen source and are instituted with stultifying regularity.

"My mother had a little pad that sat next to the telephone," says Jodi, thirty-five, "and a pencil that was the same length as the pad, and you could only use that pencil next to that pad. If you walked off with that pencil, even if you replaced it with another, she had a tantrum. Surfaces had to be clean and neat and everything had to line up. If you took a pillowcase out of the linen closet you didn't want the other pillowcases to start to lean a little bit. She would get crazed, screaming and yelling. The house was always tense, the explosion was always unexpected. I was scared to death of making a mistake."

The Controller is an expert at table manners, etiquette, bowel movements, diet, hair, dress codes, street safety, speaking manners, your silent thoughts, your secret desires, your dangerous innermost wishes. As a little girl, you try to comply. You figure that Mom knows what she is talking about. With the years, you get wiser, a little more bothered by her interference, and then you hit the rocky period of adolescence. Maybe you rebel. Maybe you retreat. The fact is, it does not matter how you react by this time. The toll has been taken. Even in your furious defiance, she has left you feeling that you cannot exist without her, that whatever you do, whichever way you turn, disaster awaits.

You rush into love affairs, marriages, crazy career choices—not because you want to or because you are following some inner desires of your own, but because you are still haunted by her voice in your head. The problem is that part of you wants to keep her voice there precisely because you have learned to depend on her rather than on yourself.

## What's Behind Mom's Behavior?

She claims that she loves you, that she is concerned with your well-being. What she is really doing is demanding that you never threaten the solutions that she believes are vital to *her* well-being. A mother whose fears are dumped on you, whose anxiety paralyzes you, who tries to deny you independence and a sense of achievement is not loving; she is scared. And she is not scared of what will happen to you, she is allowing her inner terrors to dominate her life— and yours!

For her own survival and sanity, every moment of her life is spent trying to control the chaos within her. Added to the scars from her own childhood is her unexpressed rage. Feelings are magnified when kept in the private world of fantasy, away from the possibility of being corrected by reality, and repressed rage can be extremely damaging. The Controller, constantly on the point of explosion, doesn't have the slightest idea how to handle what she is experiencing.

Everybody else thinks she is so sure of herself but the truth is otherwise. She lives in such fear that she becomes inflexible and rigidly protective. If she is in a bad marriage—as often she is—she tries to control her husband before he can control or abandon her. Since she cannot gain the kind of control she needs over her external or internal world, she looks to her daughter for the only security she can have. The contract she offers is that if you stay close and listen, do as she says, obey her every command, and allow her into every aspect of your life—she will love you always. To the child, who utterly needs her mother's love, it seems like a good deal.

This mother can have her loving moments when her inner turmoil is in check. It is easy to believe that the Controller could sit happily with her daughter in her lap, brushing and brushing until every strand of hair was compulsively set in place. Perhaps the initial desire is loving. But when the little girl begins to squirm and Mom's tension is beginning to mount, her impulses change and she is forced to say, "Just let me get a few more of these tangles undone. We don't want the neighbors to think you're a messy little girl!" Once again her love is overshadowed by inner fears. Those fears have nothing to do with the child, with the child's hair, with the neighbors' reactions. This mother is trying to control her own anxieties and emotional leftovers from her childhood.

Eventually, the daughter of the Controller cannot sit still any longer. One way or another, she gathers her resources and gets out of the passive position, or she demands to, and then the stakes are raised. By any slight declaration of independence, the daughter sets off the mother's old terrors of abandonment, which allows the possibility of danger to disrupt the mother's sense of control and safety.

## The Healthy Mother and the Toddler

The healthy mother is eminently aware of the push–pull of needs in her child. She encourages her daughter's initial forays toward independence, never threatening to remove her love as her child discovers the world on her own. Even though the good mother may have ambivalence about seeing her daughter grow up, by and large she is able to support that growth.

> Caryn, forty, mother of Jennifer, now a teenager, says, "One of the most fascinating parts of motherhood was that it gave me a chance to review my life, to see what my mother did to me, the good and the bad, and to understand better the forces that molded me. I am pretty pleased with myself at the moment because Jen turned out so terrifically but I don't remember thinking I was an especially good mom when she was an infant. Who thinks that? You just get on with it, do what you have to, you survive. There hardly ever seems to be time to figure out what's right and wrong, you work by instinct.
>
> "But once, we were in the playground when she was about three and just delighted with the speed she was beginning to pick up and the way she could fly across the ground and cover a lot of territory. She took a tumble, luckily landing on grass so she wasn't hurt,

just maybe embarrassed when she looked up and saw me and the other mothers rising out of our seats. Well, Jen picked herself up, dusted herself off, and, looking over at us with the most reassuring smile in the world, she sang, 'Silly girl!' and went about her business. I heard that lilting chant all day and it sent me to sleep at night. Any time I worried about her, I heard it again because I could never have responded that way as a child.

"She wasn't criticizing herself for making a terrible mistake. She wasn't overexaggerating the extent of the damage. She didn't feel guilty, she wasn't mortified that it had happened in front of other people. She didn't pick up the anxiety expressed by the mothers on the bench. She was able to recover from the accident, evaluate the situation, minimize the embarrassment, at the same time admitting that she had made a mistake. She had done something 'silly'—not tragic, not demeaning, not painful. She could admit it and kid herself about it and know that the world still loved her.

"Where did she learn that? I learned to howl with half-phony pain every time I scraped my knee. I learned to feel mortification every time I dropped ice cream on my shirt. Where from? From my mother's dramatic and exaggerated reactions. Somehow, Jennifer learned to take these things in her stride. I felt reassured that I was not passing on my anxiety, like my mother had done to me.

"Years later, when she was five or so, she developed a slew of imaginary playmates and loved to walk along the street in conversation with them. She also liked to pretend that she was alone. Coming home from school every day, she wanted to go by herself and I was to fol- low many steps behind. Every now and then, she might look back to see if I was there, and I would wave. She always stopped at the curb so I could keep her in my sight but people stared at this tiny tot strolling by herself on a city street. And many women would give me a dirty glance as if to say, 'How could you take such a reckless chance?' But she was clearly experimenting with being alone, albeit protected by her imaginary friends, and I knew something important was going on so I let it happen."

Sound like your mother? If your mother is a Controller, the answer is a resounding, "Not on your life!" The Controller never allows her daughter this much freedom, never encourages her to explore this way, never takes pride in her quiet times of play and discovery. The controlling mother not only wants to know what you are doing, but insists that she knows best how to do it.

## The Controller and the Toddler

The world of the infant is basically Mom and Dad: suppliers of warmth, food, love, and sensation. Though it might be nice to remain in those comforting arms, the urge to grow, to move, to find things out on our own, to discover exciting secrets like how our fingers and toes work (as well as doors and electrical outlets) is equally attractive.

Of course, there is danger. Kids get into trouble. They make messes. The more adventurous the toddler, the more the possibilities for upsets. The healthy mother sets limits, cleans up without overreacting, and teaches us to confront the world without undue fear. The controlling mother feels safe only when she is in charge and therefore has trouble fostering her child's independence.

Carol's mother demanded that everything be just so: "Children are to be seen and not heard. Always complete what you start. No jumping on the bed. Finish what is on your plate." Her mother was obsessive about her home, her appearance, table manners, etiquette, and what the neighbors would think.

"She was so busy following me around," says Carol, thirty-two, "and correcting me and keeping me supposedly safe and perfect, that the woman was able to escape her emotional emptiness for years. To this day, she talks about how happy she was as a young mother; she had a purpose, she felt fulfilled. What she means is she had power. She had a job that kept her focused and kept the demons at bay. But was she a good mother? She believed that you feed your child every three hours and don't pick her up in between.

"She did that with my son when he was a baby. I left him with her and when I got back she gloated, 'He thought he'd get the best of me but I got the best of him!' This is a one year old she's talking about! She had left him crying in a crib in a darkened room and closed the door, and I am sure she did that with me. She never once said 'I love you' that I can remember. She avoided physical contact at all costs so I learned not to expect any hugs. A good mother? This was a woman who never should have had kids in the first place—but she was one hell of a toilet trainer."

At the beginning, the daughter of the Controller goes along with Mother's wishes. She sits there and gets her hair brushed and, if she has a desire to squirm and explore, she represses that desire. She thinks she's happy because Mom is so close. She tries to stay clean, to not disrupt the household, to avoid her mother's scowl. She wants her love, she doesn't dare lose it, so it does not occur to her to question or rebel. But, boy, when the awareness of what is going on hits, when she sees how other families work, when the control becomes unbearable, the rebellion—or the desire for it—surges forth with all the years of repression giving it extra heft.

## What's in Store for the Controller's Daughter?

The Controller is a sad, unhappy, disturbed woman. But there is no way you are going to be able to help her—short of getting her into therapy herself—not by arguing with her, calling her names, trying to explain, pleading, or reasoning. No reasoning is possible here. The Controller claims to be upset by your behavior but her reactions have nothing to do with you. She claims to know how everything should be done, but her code can't be defined. It is always vague: "That's the way we did it in my day," or "That's what the neighbors will say." She claims that if you will give in on this one issue, she will be satisfied but, when she has finished criticizing your dress code, she will go onto your weight, your hair, your spouse, or your career. When you discard one boyfriend she does not like because he isn't a professional and next bring home a doctor, she will hate him because he threatens to marry you and move you far away.

But the worst part of growing up with the controlling mother is that, over the years, she becomes installed in your head. More so than the child of a healthy mother, who has encouraged independence, you don't want to lose contact with her. Being left alone feels momentous and frightening when Mother has always been there, directing and safeguarding your every move.

"She never let me in the kitchen," says Brenda, forty-three. "That was her domain. I was supposed to think—and, for years, I did—what a great mother! She'd cook it all. She'd do the table. She'd stay up till two the night before preparing and didn't want our help. 'Hey, you guys go rest!' she'd say. As a result, I developed this whole persona of the klutz so, if I tried to help, it would be a disaster. I'd spill. I'd break. I would offer to load the dishwasher and she'd say, 'It's okay. I would only have to wash the floor when you're done.' So, of course, it's always anxiety-provoking for me to do anything in the kitchen. For years, I could not understand that this was not a loving thing because that's what she said and I assumed my mother was a model of a mother! That there was anything negative to what she would do for me was mind-blowing. But the fact is that she devastated me constantly."

You're a grown woman now, you have your own life. In reality, she has no power over what you do, where you go, how you dress—yet, you, yourself, now wonder if the skirt is too short. You, yourself, question the propriety of your behavior. You see yourself as too heavy. You wonder about your abilities. You look in the mirror and see yourself as she saw you or the way, as a child, you thought she saw you. You speak and you hear her voice.

"My mom hates my boyfriend," says Danielle, who's in her twenties. "Gary is very touchy-feely so he kissed my mother on the lips first time he met her, and she was like—Whoa! Later, my father and I were arguing in a joking way and I went, 'Come on, Dad!' and Gary—this is the first time he's ever sat at our kitchen table—goes, 'Yeah, come on, Dad!' That's the way he is. My mother says, 'Oh, he's too aggressive.' Then, a week later, I said, 'You know, Gar, why don't you just be a little more gentle and not so aggressive with people?' I don't know where that came from. I had never thought he was too aggressive. I really liked that quality about him.

"I told myself what she thought didn't matter but I'd sneak him into our conversation. 'Gary came over again. Do you still not like him?' She'd say, 'It's your life. It's your life but you're not going to marry this guy. He's not right for you.' She says she wants me to make my own decisions, but she also wants me to make them her way. Meanwhile, he's enthralled with me and wants to marry me and I say, 'You know, Gary, it's not like we're married or anything. We're not going to be together forever. Why don't you back off a little?' That's her.

"I say it doesn't bother me that she doesn't like him. I'm my own person. I have to be independent. I swore to myself that I wouldn't discuss him with her any more. I bring my laundry to their house and my mother usually does it. Well, Gary sleeps over sometimes and his underwear was in my laundry pile and I forgot it was in there. My mother brought it back and I was like, 'Oh my God!' I'm twenty-four years old. I'm a woman. But I know that when she was folding his underwear, she was making all kinds of faces. I don't want to tell my mother things but, one way or the other, I do.

"This is the first real relationship I've had and I want to be able to live my own life without her controlling what I think. I left home as a way of saying, 'You can't dictate my life,' but nothing has changed. Early on, I thought Gary was wonderful and that I would love him despite what anyone could say. Now, I wouldn't marry him and fifty percent is because of my

mother. I suddenly find there's something about him
that I don't love."

## Her Voice in Your Head

What has happened here? The Controller has so dominated
her daughter's choices that, even after the daughter has left
home, she is afraid to lose her mother's approval. She
doesn't want her mother to know what is going on, yet she
"forgets" his underwear in her laundry. She wants to think
of herself as a woman, yet shouldn't a woman of twenty-
four be doing her own laundry? She clings to her mother
and maintains her dependency by incorporating her mother
into her psyche. And she loses her self.

This is a terrible bind to be in. As the daughter of a
controlling mother, you are faced with an enormous struggle to get free because you cannot trust your own
thoughts. When you are reacting to a situation, a person,
even your own image in the mirror, you do not know
whether you are expressing your desires—or hers. You say
things you don't mean. You want to do one thing yet you
behave as if you wanted something else. You feel like you
are controlled by ghosts. And worse, all the rage that
you felt but never expressed as a reaction to your mother's
control is still there. Not having expressed it makes it loom
even larger—just as your mother's unexpressed rage does
to her.

As an adult, your reaction to the situation has become complex and insidious. She is no longer the one saying that you can't call a guy you like at the office because
he will think you are man-hungry. She is not the one saying that you can't demand a raise because your boss will
think you are pushy. She is not the one criticizing and
humiliating you, you are—and rage at yourself emerges as
depression.

## Depression

Depression is more painful and difficult to handle than anger, which can be released, if only momentarily. Expressing anger can feel pleasurable and freeing. It can be directed at someone else. But depression makes it impossible to aim for higher goals. It burrows into your self-esteem, allows for no release, digs in deep, and paralyzes.

Felicia, thirty-nine years old, came into therapy because of what she described as "work-related" depression. She was a medical and scientific copy-editor, a profession that requires exacting patience and publishing know-how. In her work with technical journals, she had to rewrite articles written by academics, to charmingly persuade authors to change things, and to make sure that all the data was accurately expressed. In such a small field, it did not take long for someone who was adept at this type of work to become sought-after.

She started accepting freelance assignments to do at home after long days at her full-time job. They soon grew so overwhelming that she had to hire an assistant. Not long before she entered therapy, she had quit her job to start her own freelance editing agency, having calculated that she could quadruple her salary. In addition, she would own a business of increasing value. Her reputation assured her of getting it off the ground. She would have a great deal more control over her professional life, as well as finally winning some recognition for her talents. Even for such a sure thing, she admitted, she mulled it over for years before making the move.

Then, to her astonishment, she fell apart. She could not get herself to the desk. She could not concentrate. "I didn't dare answer the phone and say the name of the firm," she says. "I was proclaiming my competence to the world but was terrified of making some awful mistake that would appear in print and let everyone know what a fraud I was. Where was all this coming from? Here I was an expert in my field, yet I had never felt this much doubt about myself before!"

Such reactions are not uncommon when a person has made a major change. Moving out of a safe and familiar position onto new ground can be frightening. Suddenly, you are faced with the possibility of loss—and in this case, Felicia could not even define what it was she was afraid of losing. But, once she had taken the step, she could not allow herself to follow through.

After the first therapy session, Felicia found it easier to function; at least she could make it out of bed and get to the desk in the morning. It was such a relief to take action and so helpful to have somebody to talk to. The initial hurdle had been conquered.

On the surface, things got better. Even so, Felicia obsessed and all she talked about to her therapist was the new business. She felt overwhelmed by the amount of work she had accepted and was sure that she could not make the deadlines. She was impatient with her new employees, yet was unsure of herself as a boss. She did not like the efforts at sales she now had to make on her own. She lived in fear that, after the flurry of current assignments, there would be no others. At session after session, Felicia recited her woes about the firm, went over and over the obstacles before her, refused to accept the reassurances that the therapist offered, and could not move the conversation away from the office—which was a worry in itself. She still lived at home with her mother, she told the therapist, but starting the firm required that she lease office space and she stayed awake nights, convinced she could never meet the monthly rent requirements.

Well, the dreaded word—*mother!*—had finally been uttered.

The most dangerous thing about psychological pain is that it is often so intense that we have to bury it. We are convinced that the anxiety would only increase by confronting the cause, so we deny, we avoid, and—when a crisis hits and the pain surges to the surface—we blame it on something else. We obsess, talk in circles, do anything rather than get to the core of the problem and the way we are contributing to it.

"Tell me a little about your mother," said the therapist, and the floodgates opened.

"She has nothing to do with this. If you want to know the truth, she doesn't even know I've left my job. Can you believe that? I've taken this huge step and never even told her. But I knew from the first that she would worry, she would oppose me, she would try to convince me not to do it. Worse, if I had told her, she would have found some way of spreading the news to my boss or my co-workers and I would have been forced to move before I had been ready. So it started as a secret and I've kept it that way. That's how I know none of this anxiety is being caused by her, for a change."

Felicia's body language revealed the lie. When she talked about work, she was depressed, slack, lethargic. She seemed overwhelmed, her tone of voice was almost whiny, her shoulders drooped, and she avoided eye contact. Suddenly, when the subject became her mother, she sat up in her chair, her face acquired a tautness, her eyes glared, and she bit into her words. Here there was life where before there had been only numbness. The therapist encouraged her to say more about her mother.

"I think she suspects that I'm up to something new because I've had to freshen my wardrobe now that I'm meeting clients to drum up sales. Every morning we fight about what I'm wearing. She thinks my skirts are too short. She doesn't want me to wear pants—imagine!—in this day and age. She continually nags me about how much money I'm spending on clothes. Whatever the topic, we make each other nervous and holler all the time. She pries into whatever I'm doing.

"Once, she went through my bag and found a hotel key. I admit it, I had been to a hotel with a married guy and had forgotten to turn in the key. If you want the truth, that's my entire love life. I think it's disgusting myself. I don't need her to tell me I'm evil! I was furious that she had gone through my bag. I wouldn't answer any of her questions. I told her she was making me crazy and that I had decided to see a therapist. By this time, we were both in tears.

"Later that night, she woke me because she was having heart palpitations and I knew that if she died, I'd feel responsible. Also, what would I do if I didn't have a mother? You know there's somebody you can turn to if you need to, whether you want to or not. I'm the pivot of her life, but still I don't feel cared about. I would like to be able to speak to her without my gorge rising, to be more of a friend but she makes me feel that I'm ruining her life.

"I told her that I think she's crazy and that she should see a shrink. She said, 'One nut in the house is enough!' How can I deal with her? Whatever I try doesn't work. Once, I went shopping for clothes with her, figuring that if she felt included in the process, she wouldn't nag me every morning. I came home with clothes she would wear, not that I would. There's no compromise possible. It's either her way or it's wrong."

# Separation: The Next Step

As a four year old, Felicia never had the opportunity to stroll alone down the street and look back to see her mother, watching over her, yet proud of her independence. This little girl walked with her hand clutched in Mom's because they both saw the world filled with danger. Felicia had no sense that what she was experiencing was being foisted upon her, that she was being locked into a never-ending cycle. How could a four year old think that way? She needed her mother, her mother needed her; that was all she knew and in that knowledge was comfort and safety. All the tiny steps that lead us to separate from our mothers gently and gradually, that help us to find our own identities, that give us the courage to discover the world on our own were denied her; more than that, rather than find fault with her mother, she repressed any desires of her own that would lead to conflict.

Felicia built her life around the effort to retain this particular brand of connectedness—because maintaining it was gratifying to her in ways she didn't even realize. Just as she purchased clothes with her mother's sense of style, she designed a sex life that was in tune with what she thought was her mother's opinion of her.

As the relationship curdles, as the repressed forces require muffling in order to stay buried, the operatic battles that Felicia describes become a source of connectedness in themselves. The screaming, the crying, the nagging, the threats keep mother and daughter locked hand in hand as they stroll down the street. But while the pattern was started to assuage her mother's internal sense of chaos, that sense of chaos is now shared by Felicia as well.

It will take months, even years, before Felicia is able to comprehend the connection between her obsessive fears about work and her relationship with her mother. As she does, she might be able to make tentative moves toward independence. Generally, an awareness that problems with her mother have crept into every corner of her life is necessary before a daughter can fully commit to making changes.

If the first step in resolving problems with your mother is that you must learn to see your relationship clearly, the second step is to look at the way the past is invading the present. Once confronted, horrifying feelings from the past can be dealt with. But if these feelings remain buried, they will poison any real affection that you have for your mother, as well as potentially cripple you for the rest of your life.

## Strategies for Change

- Learn to look. The major obstacle to "seeing" is that your fear of change is so great, you refuse to see. You convince yourself that everything is fine with Mom, yet your love life falls apart. You cannot function at work, are plagued with irrational fears, fall into a rage over some innocuous mistake your daughter has made, explode at the bank teller when something she says sets off signals from the past, worry incessantly, say things you do not mean, lose track of your purpose in life. In defiance, you become excessively self-reliant. You fear that others will seek to control you like Mom did so you isolate yourself.

- Stop obsessing about the symptoms. If you are overweight, are having trouble with men, are not succeeding in your career, are prone to depression or a sense of aimlessness, put these aside for a moment. If your relationship with your mother is at the core of these difficulties, then the surface problems are only a screen. Stop concentrating on the immediate crises, stop staying up at night and berating yourself for what you are doing wrong. Stay calm. Try to keep your present anxieties at bay, acknowledging that it might be necessary to dig deeper in order to discover real causes and solutions.

- Concentrate on the present. You need to understand the past but you cannot expect to change it. Don't revive old memories so that you can wallow in self-pity. Do not phone and yell at your mother for what happened twenty years ago. She won't have the slightest idea what you are talking about. If you find yourself using phrases like "You always . . ." when you are arguing with her, stop. You are drifting into history. The longer you remain focused on the past, with what she didn't do, what you didn't get, the less you are going to be able to look clearly at the present and the less you are going to be able to change things.

- Stop working on automatic pilot. When you get off the phone with her, even when things go well, start thinking over what happened. Try to form a picture of the patterns in your relationship. Do the same at work with other reactions that are routine and have nothing to do with what you truly feel. If you do something that pleases her, not you, and then feel humiliated and end up raiding the refrigerator—and if this is standard procedure—try to catch it right after it happened. What did she say? How did you respond? Why did you do that? These everyday interchanges are often the best clues to how your relationship with your mother works and what it is costing you.

- Form a better picture of who your mother really is. Ask her about her life. Get her to share memories. Dig into family history. Pore through photos. Question relatives about their recollections of her as a girl. Try to understand who she was—who she is—separate from you. A valuable experiment is to try to listen to her as you would a friend, someone you are not enmeshed with. Ask yourself, "Who is this person?" Investigate the possible motives behind her behavior. They won't make it easier to forgive her, they are not a justification, but they can help you to understand.

- Try to see the good as well as the bad. Some of the things she tried to teach you are of value, some of her rules made sense, some of the habits you inherited have turned out to be helpful. If she wasn't truly responsive to you, maybe she was to a sister or a brother, or at her job or maybe she was admirable when battling with a cop over a traffic ticket. If she wasn't a terrific homebody, perhaps you can admire her intellectual achievements. They might not have been what you needed when you were growing up but, now that you are an adult, perhaps you can respect other areas of her functioning. You might even see how you have inherited those talents and admire yourself a bit more.

- Cease envying your girlfriends for their great relationships with their mothers. It is not helpful to dream about how your problems would be solved if only your college professor had been your mom. Your mother is your mother and she's all you've got. You are not going to improve the relationship if you cling to impossible ideals.

Maybe you two are never going to have the close, loving friendship that you want; this does not mean you have to exclude her from your life forever. You'll have to settle for the best relationship that can be successfully managed. It might never fulfill your fantasies, but you are better off working toward limited goals than living in perpetual disappointment.

# 3

# The Yenta

## *The Preteen Develops a Self*

*D*inah, in her early twenties, worked for a big auction house and was assigned to top-secret negotiations when Barbra Streisand was thinking of putting her art and antiques on the block. It was a big step up for Dinah, who had spoken to Streisand's representatives and was set to fly to California. In her excitement, she told her mother, warning her that if news leaked out beforehand, the house might lose the assignment.

> On her return to the office after the trip, Dinah was besieged with calls from her cousins and her mother's friends and neighbors, asking what Barbra was really like! Her mother couldn't understand Dinah's rage. "I did it because I'm proud of you! What's wrong with that?"

"Not only had she jeopardized the deal and my job,"
says Dinah, "but it's so demeaning. It's a way of taking
the achievement away. Nothing is private. Nothing gives
pleasure simply because it is—everything becomes fod-
der for her luncheons with the ladies. It's a way for her to
get the glory, not for me to shine. Most of the time, her
damned stories are better than my achievements! She
makes my life more interesting and glamorous than it is.
After all, I never did meet Barbra. So, in the end, I feel less
valued—not more—and, to top it off, I have to apologize
for her lies."

## Qualities of the Yenta

The Yenta—an old Yiddish expression for a gossip—dines
out on any or all of your accomplishments as if they were
hers and, in so doing, steals them.

There is another danger with this kind of mother, as
twenty-seven-year-old Kathy describes it:

"I had lost my job and my life was in the pits. My mom
went to Hawaii and when she returned she said to me,
'I didn't call while I was away so as not to ruin my vacation. I couldn't even go down to dinner in my hotel since
you left me nothing to talk about!'"

The message from Mom is clear: Everything depends on
what other people think. No achievement, no effort, no
desire is valued for its own sake by the Yenta; nothing is
private, nothing is safe. Every moment of your life is set out
on the front porch to be evaluated by the neighbors; only
when they approve will praise be forthcoming from Mom.

"My mother is a very social woman so everywhere I go it's, 'Oh, you're Gail Burney's daughter!'" says Cheryl, twenty-four. "I grew up as 'Gail Burney's daughter' and everybody knew my business. At my brother's wedding, everybody said, 'So we hear what's going on with you. You're very happy, you're at school. Your job is good.' I didn't have to say a word, everybody already knew. That kind of blew me away.

"I overhear her on the phone saying, 'No, she's not seeing anybody now.' Whose business is that? Recently, I went on a blind date. Somebody called me and I had no idea what the connection had been, how he got my name, but it definitely led one way or another, four people removed, to my mother—who gave my number to somebody else who gave it to her son's friend. What right did she have to do that?

"Another time, I was dating a guy from my home-town and she was furious because I wouldn't tell her his name. My mother is very impressed with backgrounds. Her first question when I meet a new guy is, 'So what does the father do?' And I knew she would do a whole background check on this one. Not only what his father does, but what clubs his parents belong to, what his golf handicap is . . . She would find out who his last girlfriend was. And everybody else would find out, too!

"Every year we go to temple on the Jewish High Holy Days, and every year I say to myself, 'I can't stand this.' All it is is a fashion show and I'm going because my parents want everybody to see that we are a family. Every year she buys me a brand-new outfit and, right after services get out, we have to stand outside for half an hour to kiss everybody hello. If I said I'm not going, she'd never speak to me again.

"I've never wanted to be known as a person whose relationship with her mother has irretrievably broken down. I know a few people who are estranged from their parents and they carry around a stigma. I don't want her friends, our relatives to think of me like that. I never liked that image."

This is a woman who is so conflicted about separating from her mother that she can't do it without worrying about what everybody else will think!

## What's Behind Mom's Behavior?

The good mother values your dreams as well as your achievements. She values *you,* not your production, and in this valuing she teaches you to value yourself as well. The Yenta uses your achievement to fulfill her own needs for attention, for acclaim, for identity. "She doesn't see me!" is the constant complaint of the daughter of the Yenta.

"Even if I do something wonderful, the point isn't that I'm so terrific, but isn't she a terrific mother!" A painful part of the Yenta's mechanism is that she refuses to value your achievements according to your standards. What pleases *you* is not important; what matters is only how it will look to her community, according to her standards.

"I was very prim and proper in high school," says Gillian, twenty-one. "Skirts, sweaters, trim-fitting pants. When I went to college, it was flannel shirts, jeans, hiking boots. My mother would ask, 'When are you going to become a girl again?' Then she went crazy because she was convinced that one of my male friends at school was gay and, one time, we were on the phone and the conversation turned to a girlfriend of mine who is a lesbian. My mother said something derogatory and I cried, 'Ma!' She immediately said, 'Gillian, are you a lesbian?' I told her no but she couldn't leave it at that.

"When she came up to our sorority house on Visiting Day, I had been elected Phi Lam Fairy. Everybody had a nickname and mine meant that I was the nicest sister. I wasn't going to haze anybody during pledging. Everyone loved me. I was so proud and excited that my name was up on the board. I showed it to her and could tell instantly that something was wrong. She looked around as if she would die if anybody saw and whispered to me, 'What exactly does Phi Lam Fairy mean?' It spoiled the whole day for me; it spoiled having the nickname which had meant so much."

To the Yenta, your value depends on how you aggrandize her—and on other people's applause—something which diminishes your every achievement. Only if you bring the Yenta rewards will you be rewarded. You grow up measuring yourself by this standard and then, unfortunately, you relate to friends, to teachers, to lovers, to husbands, and to your children this way.

## The Healthy Mother and the Preteen

Through early interaction with her parents, particularly her mother, a girl gets to know herself. The healthy mother validates the girl's hopes and feelings. She listens, helping her daughter to sort through what she is experiencing, giving her daughter's reactions a legitimacy. Even differences between the two are handled with respect.

As the girl grows, she becomes a woman who values her impulses, who knows what she wants, who can listen to her inner voice, who knows where she ends and others begin. She can assert her opinions when they are different from others. Although she has conflicts, she is not paralyzed by them. This lucky person has a central core of feelings, attitudes, and beliefs to depend on. She does not have to seek approval from others for her likes, her dislikes, or her choices in life. She does not depend on the opinions of others for a definition of who she is.

Throughout the girl's formative years, a true inner self should be forming in the continual decisions she makes about what she likes and what she doesn't, who she is and who she is not. As a toddler, she performs by rote and imitation. After the age of about seven, she becomes involved in school activities that offer the possibilities of mastering new challenges, of learning what she can achieve, of trying out different identities. Her curiosity about sexuality heightens. She gets more deeply involved with peer groups, with cliques, with "best" friends, with organized games that place heavy emphasis on rules.

She develops crushes on teachers and women other than her mother who are models of who she wants to be and what she wants to accomplish. This important developmental step helps her to see her mother more objectively, to compare her to other women, and to have options for herself. Her own development is facilitated by supportive women who've achieved the goals that she is striving for. The girl emulates their attitude toward themselves and learns new ways to solve problems. In addition, she can appreciate other women in a way she cannot appreciate her mom.

**"My Aunt Peggy lived down the hall from us," says Gwen, forty-five. "She was my mother's sister but they couldn't have been more different. Peggy was charming,**

cheerful, non-judgmental. Her apartment was total chaos. Never in her life had she put a spoon away. You could leave the bread on the bed and she wouldn't care; she didn't know where it belonged anyway. My mother's apartment was immaculate, with lots of fancy furniture, all for show. But she was so busy keeping up a front that, when I was a Girl Scout and we needed a troop leader, Peggy did it because my mother didn't have time.

"I would go down the hall and disappear into Peggy's cozy household where she was always puttering about, growing her plants or something. She didn't talk much, two sentences was as much as she'd say—but you always felt you'd had a conversation. My mother talked incessantly—on the phone to friends, babbling to me—but there was never space for me to respond. With Peggy, I could chat about school, moan about science class. And she listened! My mother never listened.

"What's strange is that, nowadays, Peggy's kids complain that she never cooked, never worried about what they wore. They were mortified that the house was such a mess. They remember her as being neglectful. It's funny, but when you separate a woman from her power over you as a mother, you can enjoy the good parts and ignore the bad. That's what was so valuable about having an aunt like Peggy."

The preteen girl develops a feminine gender role and a valued body image. She plays around with showing off—with running, dancing, tumbling—to seek praise for her body. Little by little, she makes sense of the world. But this is a private journey and it should not be intruded upon. It cannot happen if a mother is constantly hovering. Essential to the establishment of a sense of well-being is a mother's ability to safeguard periods in which a child can just "be."

Finally, an inner voice begins to develop. The girl learns to rely on it more than on the opinions of others; she grows familiar with it and seeks it out in solitude. She gets in touch with her feelings. Healthy self-esteem comes from a sense of her own effectiveness, of her ability to make things happen, not just from her mother's praise.

As an adult, this girl will someday have the quiet assurance that she is more than a wife, a mother, a girlfriend. She is more than a dancer, a lawyer, an editor. These are roles and, though she cannot live in society without them, she also knows that roles change. So do goals. So do relationships and, when they do, it is only the inner self that will get her through. The healthy woman has had these early years to acquaint herself with her private and independent existence, separate from everything and everyone around her.

## The Yenta and the Preteen

"I was the first child and the first grandchild," says Samantha, thirty-one, "and I recall being the center of attention, but I also remember dark sides to that attention. My mother wanted me to be 'the prettiest and the best' and, since I was not allowed to have an opinion different from hers, I went along with the program.
I read early and skipped grades. At dinner parties, I was called to the table and asked to recite poetry.

"I resisted once and Mom called me a little fool and dismissed me from the room, which was devastating! I've only remembered recently how she used to pinch as a punishment—if I made a mistake while reciting, for instance. It really hurt but I never complained. I just tried harder.

"My response was to become an achiever. I went to a well-known college where I felt out of my depth, but my mother was pleased, my grandparents were impressed, so I told myself that I was happy. Very early on, I learned to ignore my own feelings.

"When I was about ten, I developed eating problems and played hooky from school. Still, my mother and my aunt—to this day—talk about me as such a sunny child! As an adolescent, I felt ugly and unattractive. I had no boyfriends at all, just boys who were 'friends'—a fate worse than death. Still, I never expressed any unhappiness because I was so busy 'producing' for others.

"I still want people to think I'm attractive and nice, so I can't make a decision that would upset a soul. Like what movie would I want to see? I don't even think how I feel about it; rather, I am focused on how would so-and-so like me to feel about it?

"What's funny is that everybody envied me as a child, everybody told me how wonderful my parents were and no one was listening to me! The anguish and frustration started a long time ago and I'm only just acknowledging it. Up to now, I've been walking through life like an impostor. My mother loved to take me clothes shopping and dress me up for special occasions. 'My little doll!' she used to call me and I was always pleased. But a doll is not real! A doll is something that can be put down when you get tired of playing with it. Yeah, I'm her little doll, but a doll is made of plastic."

A little doll is missing a self: that innermost core made up of your feelings, your desires, your history, your needs, your memories. It is who you truly are, separate from your roles, your career, your achievements, even your relationships. Your sense of the world should be an accurate reflection of everything you have gone through in life and how you felt and thought about it all. Religions call this the soul. Psychoanalysis calls it the self. Without a sense of self, we cannot develop, we cannot relate, we cannot grow.

## The Authentic Self Versus the False Self

If you've been brought up trying to please a Yenta, whose only objective is to impress the outside world, you'll quickly learn to stifle aspects of yourself. You'll develop a facade, a way of being in the world that has nothing to do with your feelings. You'll find it difficult to value independent achievement if it doesn't fit in with your mother's definition of success—even if the achievement is valued by everyone else in the world!

> Lydia, age twenty-eight, is on her way to a Ph.D., yet, she says, "My mother doesn't care about school. All she wants is for me to marry. She doesn't even care if I love the guy. Love and happiness are not important, she says. She doesn't care what I'm like inside. All that's important is that I marry a doctor or a lawyer, just so she can say that I married well."

Lydia can see that her mother's values are askew but, despite the fact that she can find support for the direction she is taking from any number of sources, she feels inadequate.

Therapists differentiate between the *authentic* self and the *false* self. For example, the daughter of the Yenta cannot rely on her own emotions. She has no sense of her real needs, doesn't value her own thoughts, doesn't follow through on her impulses because she has developed a self that depends primarily on someone outside herself. She does only what will gain approval, reveals only what is expected of her, develops a masked view of herself, and eventually fuses so totally with that mask that she loses touch with the remainder of her being. This is alienation from the authentic self to the highest degree. The only thing that exists, even to the young woman herself, is that false front.

Drew Barrymore, who started working at eleven months, was a star by seven, and had become a cocaine addict at twelve, writes:

> Someone once explained to me what the word
> *veneer* meant. Gloss. A shiny surface that's supposed
> to protect an inferior material underneath. That's me
> exactly.[1]

The child who is loved for her achievements rather than herself becomes a woman who feels that she has to earn love by pleasing; yet that kind of love is never adequate because it is offered only to the self that complies with what Mother wants. So the cycle is unending because the true self never receives the loving that it requires.

If you constantly seek validation from the outside world, if you have no faith in your thoughts and feelings, if you are not connected with what you are actually experiencing, then you cannot trust any love. Because you are totally dependent on external reactions, you will always need more confirmation.

---

1. Drew Barrymore and Todd Gold, *Little Girl Lost* (New York: Pocket Books, 1990), p. 8.

# What's in Store for the Yenta's Daughter?

No matter how successful the daughter of the Yenta becomes—and she is often a high achiever because she has been so geared to production—her success does not reach down to her feelings. This kind of success can be meaningless. Despite all the raises, promotions, titles, acclaim, she often feels empty and worthless. To others, she seems tense and brittle; some people describe her as "without depth."

In *My Mother/My Self,* Nancy Friday writes:

> Instead of success I could believe in, I went after
> success other people believed in. I got my reward
> from other people's opinion of me . . . I was a
> successful, sexual, professional woman. I knew my
> shabby secret . . .[2]

Friday's secret is the jealous, insecure child beneath this smooth facade, a child obsessed with fear of loss.

The Yenta's daughter becomes a compulsive "doer"; always busy, cleaning, sewing, shopping so that she doesn't have to stop and discover how frightened and alone and empty she feels.

She relinquishes her rights of independence and freedom of speech. Meek and adaptive, she tolerates all kinds of exploitation and does not even recognize how much she resents those she empowers. Instead, she feels numb and constantly depressed. She goes to any lengths to rationalize her mother's behavior and is confused by her own feelings about her.

---

2. Nancy Friday, *My Mother/My Self: The Daughter's Search for Identity* (New York: Delacorte Press, 1977), pp. 297–298.

## Loss of Creativity

A serious loss to the woman with a false self is in the area of creativity. Only if there is a connection between your internal world and your actions can creativity flourish. And the more it flourishes, the more you understand and experience that internal world. If you are not in touch with your feelings, if you are afraid of your impulses, you have stifled your sensitivity, awareness, and empathy. You have put a lid on the possibility of expressing yourself—and you have suffered a great loss.

The daughter of the Yenta is not interested in originality but in producing something that pleases others. She is a conformist who can't allow her thoughts to flow without fear of the outside world intruding. But the need to communicate one's inner life is the impulse of any healthy individual and, if creativity is eliminated, one's sense of joy, fun, spontaneity, expression, confidence, and sharing is severely compromised.

Miranda, thirty-three, took a painting course and was astonished by what she saw. "All I could do were delicate and pretty things in good taste. That wasn't what I was like inside at all. I couldn't believe I had done them; it was like I was smothering myself with this 'nice person' character. I guess I'd be devastated if someone looked at a picture of mine and thought I was mean or cruel.

"I postpone returning something to a store," says Miranda. "After all, what will they think? It's not ladylike. A lady is quiet, not aggressive. She crosses her legs and has clean fingernails, speaks properly, doesn't get angry. My mother always said, 'No matter what anyone does to you, always behave like a lady.' It went without saying that it was not ladylike to express my needs. As a result,

I've lost myself in the superficial. How can I ever expect to be an artist when my work reveals how fraudulent I am as a person?"

## Difficulty Making Decisions

The woman hiding behind a false self is even more distant from her feelings than the person in conflict. She functions—perhaps even expertly—on automatic pilot. Everything in her life is superficial and carefully controlled, designed to appease the world as she has come to know it. The result is not anger, not resentment, not an urgent desire to change but emptiness, deadness, depression—and an inability to know what she wants.

> Bonnie, thirty-seven, lived with a man for four and a half years even though, she says, "After two weeks, my gut knew it was a bad situation. I gnawed on the decision like a dog on a bone. If I could have slept thirteen hours a day, I would have. Clean up the house? Forget it! I suffered constant psychic exhaustion and it wasn't the lousy guy that was draining me. It was my inability to make up my mind about what to do about him! Finally, my sister forced me to leave but, on my own, I wasn't able to move and nothing could make me happy. Then I was miserable and humiliated because I hadn't made the decision—she had."
>
> Bonnie was in trouble long before she met this man. She had always been hesitant about even the smaller moves in life. "I never know what to eat. If I try to pick an ice cream flavor, I'm forever holding up lines because I can't decide, which only makes everybody angry and that makes it harder for me. Most of the time, I walk out

without picking anything because I feel people peering over my shoulder. But then, I end up with nothing and my friends get so annoyed they stop inviting me to go places!"

Often what makes decisions difficult is the desire, somewhere deep inside, to remain a child. This desire is rooted in the wish to remain with Mother and the fear of separating from her. The conflict makes a dilemma of easy decisions because it is the act of deciding itself, rather than the decision, that is the real problem. To decide is the province of the grown-up; to have someone or something else decide for you is the position of a child. If you are having a lot of trouble making decisions, you may want to think about whether you have hidden investments in remaining your mother's child.

"In college, I went to buy a futon," says Bonnie. "I must have looked in forty stores. Finally, I picked one that cost about a hundred dollars. Actually, I had seen it early on but had been afraid to buy it. 'Well,' I mumbled, 'it's expensive but I'll have it for the rest of my life.' It had never dawned on me that I wouldn't have to live with the same futon forever!"

If you start small, step by step, you can conquer your anxiety about making decisions. Investigate your anxiety like a scientist. Set up your own experiments. If you obsess about which color lipstick to use every morning, for a few days intentionally pick the "wrong" one. You'll learn that you can survive. You'll learn that everything does not depend on a single decision, that a mistake is not going to bring you the humiliation you fear. Your anxiety comes from the past. Your relationship with your Yenta mother is blocking every turn.

"You can develop a new set of muscles to take risks and the smaller issues are a good place to start," says Dr. Audrey Amdursky, director of psychological services at the Juilliard School. "Eventually you get to the point of recognizing we are on this earth, we have a certain amount of time, we have some choices to make, and we all do the best we can. What do I want? Can I answer that question without being perfect? You will learn that you will continue whether you make the right decision or not."

# Separation: Finding Your Inner Voice

The best decisions are the ones that seem to make themselves; they simply unfold before you. Your inner voice will tell you what to do if you are enough at peace that you can hear it. This does not mean that you won't ever make wrong choices, but you will not end up humiliated by them. You will not spend years punishing yourself and growing even more frightened. You will not end up feeling like a child because you got swayed by someone else's advice, because you acted in a way that you thought would please others rather than yourself. People who listen to their inner self manage to pick themselves up, start all over, and learn from the experience.

The first time that you hear your inner voice you will know that you have gotten in touch with something that is truly you. It is different from everyone else's voice; different from all the expectations placed upon you. It takes calm to hear your inner voice as well as patience, faith, and some distance from your mother before the right path will be revealed.

Dale, thirty-two, gives this example: "I married right out of high school, a big mistake, mainly to appease my mom. We had a huge wedding and I hated every minute of it, but I remember gritting my teeth and thinking, 'This is her wedding, not mine!' The marriage ended quickly and I swore I would never marry again. For ten years, I didn't even think about it. Then I met Jay and didn't want to lose him, but I couldn't make up my mind to marry him either, because I so mistrusted the pressure I was getting from my mother who, of course, was immediately planning another blow-out.

"Finally, I decided to get away and went to Europe to a lot of the spots I had been to on my whirlwind honeymoon—places filled with such expectation and eventual disappointment. In Rome I visited a girlfriend, and all I could feel was that it was so cold in that apartment. She had never married and was alone and it was so cold! On the plane coming back, I could feel Jay's warmth enveloping me as I got closer and closer to home and suddenly was sure I wanted to marry him and that it was my decision, nobody else's. I had actually known what I had wanted all along, I suppose, but for the first time, I received my own signals. He was there at the airport and we ran away and were married within a week!"

It was not until Dale took the trip that she gave herself a chance to check out her own feelings. She finally mourned the death of her first marriage, felt the regret, got past her anger with her mother, and acknowledged how much she wanted to be with Jay. Perhaps the distance of the trip allowed her to open herself up to her inner voice and to hear what it was saying. But physical distance is not the only way you can gain perspective.

Spending time alone, thinking and feeling, not pressuring yourself to decide, not overloading the process with anxiety—nurtures the discovery of what you truly wish to do. But how do those who have no experience in allowing this to happen ever get there?

"Instead of sticking to peanut butter and jelly," says Dr. Amdursky, "move on to a chicken salad sandwich. Be angular. Build up muscle and strength and the courage to take the risk. Often, we have to do something different in order to find ourselves. Learn to trust yourself, know enough about yourself to move. One of the ways is to make small decisions and find out that the consequences are not so great. Stop worrying about whether you are pleasing everybody else. Let's get back to you. The more risks you take, the more likely you are to get in touch with what you want."

## Strategies for Change

- Learn to make small decisions first: what to wear, where to have dinner, whether or not to cut your hair. It is inevitably true that those who have learned to trust themselves on the minor issues have an easier time with the large ones. Remember that in very few instances in life is there just one "right" or "wrong" choice. However, by not making a decision, or by letting your mother (or mother substitutes) make it for you, it is sure to be the wrong one. If you quickly select the "wrong" restaurant, the evening will still go more smoothly than if you have burdened it with the tension of a drawn-out choice.
- Learn to follow your impulses. You are probably afraid of jumping in and making a decision, of failure, of disappointing others, of humiliation—you are afraid you will have to live with the consequences of the wrong move forever. Think this over carefully. How many choices in life are that important and everlasting? Not what flavor ice

cream to pick! In most cases, even the wrong decision can be corrected. You can always go back to where you started. It is necessary to learn to follow your impulses because, once you get into the rut of denying them, paralysis seeps through your entire life.

- Notice how you feel. The daughter of the Yenta tends to shrug off disappointment and hurt because she is afraid of her own emotions. If a friend gets upset because she has been treated badly by somebody else and you have been treated in the same way by that person but didn't even respond—notice that, question that.

- Concentrate on "being" instead of "doing." If you are uncomfortable when you are not doing anything, investigate that. If you turn on the T.V. every time you enter the house, if you get anxious when you are not involved in an activity, it is a clue that you are not in touch with your authentic self.

- Start exploring your own thoughts and feelings. This is going to be difficult because much of what will emerge will not fit into the framework you have created for your life. Many of the feelings will seem "unacceptable" because you will immediately judge them in your mother's voice. But she is not in the room, so dig deeper. Many women find only negative feelings at first—anger, resentment, hatred, envy. Hang onto them. While anger is not the only feeling you are searching for, it can be the first authentic one you will unearth. The pleasure you will experience in finally feeling it will help you to look for what else has been buried.

- Free your authentic self through meditation, prayer, or creativity. Many women find that a good way to start the search is by keeping a journal, which allows you to explore and to differentiate your feelings. If you are hanging around the house in your bathrobe, regrouping after a tough week, and your mother phones to barrage

you with questions, demands, and worries that a neigh-
bor is going to drop by and see you in this state, don't
explode. Get off the phone and write down what
you feel.

- Name your feelings. Intruded upon? Caught? Guilty?
Shamed? Naming your feelings provides a moment of
recognition and delay in which you can define your discomfort. It gives you a chance to handle them other than
through denial or an outburst. Are you disappointed,
frustrated, envious, defeated? Naming the specific feeling
to yourself—not generalizing it—can help you formulate
ways to deal with it.

- Learn to accept your whole self. Try to accept sexual
thoughts and feelings and aggressive impulses as a therapist would—without judging them as bad or unacceptable, but as part of being human. Desires that we grow
up condemning are part and parcel of a healthy development. We may not want to act on them but they need to
be acknowledged as part of us. What feels gigantic and
destructive to a child takes its place in the scheme of
things when looked at by an adult. This kind of searching
can be done in a journal and it can lead you to your
authentic self.

- Learn to separate from the distractions of your day and
reduce your tensions by deep breathing or exercise.
Making contact with your true desires, your needs, your
dreams is a very slow process but, as your true self begins
to be heard, you'll start to rely on it more than you do the
opinions of others, you'll seek out solitude rather than
the social whirl. Runners talk about the "high" they feel,
the joy in digging deep and experiencing only the
moment. Women who meditate talk about the bliss of
overcoming the physical discomforts—the pain of sitting
for so long with a straight back, without moving no matter
how you feel. In intense exercise as well as meditation,

you harness all your senses and overcome the difficulties and then "click in"; you plug into an inner energy that is exclusively yours yet connects you to everything else in the universe.

- Whatever your method for self-exploration, do not tell your mother! She is not going to be able to help you on this quest. If you do tell her, she'll be on the phone in twenty minutes and you'll hear from aunts and cousins: "What's happening to you? Are you going crazy? Your mother says you're turning Buddhist or something!" or worse yet, "How wonderful that you're becoming spiritual! Your mom is so proud of you!"

Psychotherapist Florence Miller Radin says, "Daughters who confide secret personal or professional information to mothers who have a compulsive need to tell all in order to make themselves interesting are like adults who let small children play with matches and think that saying 'Be careful' will protect them. The lesson is, Do not give your mother, or others, any information they are not capable of handling appropriately."

This is certainly true if you have decided there is something wrong with your life and are setting out to explore what it is. This is a private journey and, no matter how anxious it makes you, don't look for confirmation or release or approval from anyone else. You have already wasted too much of your life doing just that.

# 4

# The Smother Mother

## *The Early Teen's Anger and Rebellion*

S he worries about you. She's overprotective. Every wonderful new thing that happens in your life sets off her alarms; not, she will claim, because she is jealous or frightened—oh no, she is only concerned for you.

### Qualities of the Smother Mother

"When I was hitting my teens," says thirty-year-old Nora, "I remember getting furious at my mother, blasting off at her about something she was doing, and she would rush forward, wrap me in her arms, press me to her breasts, and sigh, 'Don't say that, my little darling. Don't you know how much Mommy loves you?' I would stay there, unable to breathe, and think, 'Why does she always tell me how much she loves me? What does that have to do with anything?'"

Mimi, twenty-seven, was an up-and-coming designer and all she heard from her mom was: "You're working too hard. You're working those hours? You're never going to get married at this rate!"

"I suppose she's terrified that I'll become a stranger because my life is moving in a different direction," says Mimi. "She wants to own me, she needs to know every detail of my life. She would celebrate if I moved back home and, for all her carrying on about my marrying, she is ambivalent whenever I meet a man because he might take me away from her.

"All she seems to want is for me to travel the safest route—but what she's really after is for my life to be exactly like hers, certainly not better! 'If you could only be like your cousin, Joanie,' she says. In my eyes, Joanie is the world's biggest bore! But Joanie is an expert bridge player, just like my mother, and they are both convinced I am doomed to loneliness because I don't play. Mom can't imagine any life other than her own, which is bad enough, but what makes me even angrier is that she's doing it because any success I might have in changing things would threaten her existence."

The Smother Mother cleans your room and throws out things you meant to keep. When you object to the intrusion, she proclaims, "What did I look at? What was I looking for? The room was a mess; I realize you're busy. I was only trying to help. Don't you see how much I love you?"

How can you respond by telling her what you feel? Her identity is centered around the role of a loving mother and she will admit no other motives.

"I had the flu," Mimi continues. "She hears the raspiness in my voice over the phone and, two hours later, she's at my door, loaded down with grocery bags. She hadn't asked, she hadn't said she was coming over, and I had plenty of food in the house and just wanted to sleep. As usual, I didn't dare say what I felt. So I let her in and, as she showed off what she had bought, we quibbled over every item. Things came to a ridiculous head when she unpacked a six-pack of Coke. Somebody had told her that carbonated soda was good for a cold, but she brought caffeine-free Coke, which I hate, so I lit into her: 'I never drink caffeine-free! Take it back. Don't you dare leave it here!' Her face crumbles, the tears start to well. I feel guilty—and rightly so. Here this woman has dragged shopping bags to me, and a six-pack of Coke is not light, and now I'm insisting she take it back.

"What I'm saying, as I'm saying it, makes me feel awful, and to cover up my guilt I go on about how insensitive she is to my needs, and if I'd wanted her to bring Coke I would have asked, and it was a stupid old wives' tale anyway that Coke is good for a cold because the truth is that it rips away the lining of your guts—or some other old wives' tale that I've heard. She doesn't give up so easily. 'You always drink caffeine-free coffee at my house,' she explains. 'What do I know about the difference? I only know what you drink at my house.' Blah, blah, blah. Then I attack back, 'I only drink caffeine-free coffee in your house because that's all you have. For years, I've put up with what you want instead of what I want in terms of coffee and now you insist on spreading what you want into my Coke! Take it out of here!'

"So, she picks up the six-pack but instead of saying, 'Don't you know how much I love you?' something comes out of her mouth that shocks us both. 'Well, to hell with you, then,' she hisses—and we're both astonished that this stupid argument should come to this. I'm so devastated and upset and weakened that I get dizzy and she has to lead me to bed and stay to make tea and toast, and then we're together all day, nobody mentions the argument, the both of us are shell-shocked. Finally, she leaves—the six-pack sitting triumphantly on the table—and I weep all night!"

## The Worrier: Variation on a Theme

Tessa, age twenty-nine, says, "My mother is always worried about me. Even when things are going smoothly, there is this note of hysteria in her voice. It sounds like she's screaming over the phone. 'Ma, I can hear you,' I'm always saying. She says she worries because she loves me so much. So what is she so worried about? She calls me five times in two days and always asks the same question, 'Did ya eat?' As if I'm an infant! When I can't stand it any more, I say, 'To tell the truth, last night I didn't feel like cooking so I had Häagen-Dazs and potato chips.' It's like a stab in her heart but at least it shuts her up!

"Then I feel guilty. So I end up calling back, apologizing, explaining, eventually making a date to come over for dinner so she can make sure I'm not starving! I tell her I'm on a diet, no starches, and she prepares french fries. By this time, I'm so upset, I eat everything she serves and keep quiet for fear of what other awful things I might say."

Strangely enough, Tessa castigates herself as angry, rebellious, and mean. She says, "When I was a kid, I wished she would die so I could be free. I never learned to communicate because I was so afraid my resentment would come out and be seen. I was secretive, good, a quiet listener because if I ever took the spotlight, I would be exposed."

As an adult, Tessa fears to be on her own and Mom fears to release her. Tessa cannot risk telling her mom the truth about what she feels so it comes out in bitchy stabs. She never confronts directly. Then she feels guilty and relapses into a child's voice, querulous tones, evasive attacks. Grown women do not behave this way. When asked a question, they give a straight answer. They state their demands directly. They are not afraid the other person will become angry at their candor.

"It is difficult to be clear with my mother because I am so angry at her and I feel so guilty about my anger," Tessa says. "I worry that if I say what I mean, all hell will break loose."

## What's Behind Mom's Behavior?

The Smother Mother is, in many cases, a woman with no identity other than that of Mother. If she had a career, if she had a sense of herself and an independent existence outside of the home, if she had a satisfying marriage with a partner who appreciated her, she might not need to invest so much of herself in motherhood. Whatever the cause, the core of her life is empty—except for her daughter—so, rather than dealing with her own emptiness, she absorbs herself in the child and interprets this absorption as love.

If the Smother Mother allowed her true feelings to surface, they would threaten the structure of her life, her marriage, and her self-concept. She denies anger in herself and will have no truck with hostility. She does not acknowledge any unhappiness and she will not allow you to do so either.

In her suffocation of any dark or negative expression of feelings, she does not allow you room to breathe, to be honest, to find a voice of your own. In order to cut off the possibility that you will say something hostile, she *tells* you what you are feeling, what you should feel, and what you shouldn't.

## The Healthy Mother and the Early Teen

Conflict between an adolescent daughter and her mother is inevitable, natural, and healthy. After all, the daughter is staking out her claims to autonomy and independence. Her struggles are monumental. She grapples with who she is, what she believes, what she looks like, what her powers are in the world, what limits she has to respect, and what barriers she can break. How does a child figure this out? She plays roles, trying out hairdos, body piercing, nail colors, and dress styles. She experiments with different ways of speaking, for example, holding her hands and giggling like a popular girl in her class.

She does not know whether she likes the giggle, whether she wants to giggle like that, or even whether she can carry it off, so she tries it at home where she has always rehearsed before exposing herself to the outside world. Of course, the new giggle comes out strangely and her mother whirls about as if some gargoyle has invaded her daughter's body.

"What was that?" she gasps.

And the daughter explodes. "That's just like you! Every time you hear something different, something new, perhaps a little sophisticated, you put it down!"

SLAM! She's off to her room and probably won't appear again (at least until dinner) but her blaring music will let everyone know she's furious. When the music stops, her sobbing will be heard. Her mother, befuddled, slightly ashamed of herself, questioning her own existence, and feeling hurt and deserted, also starts to cry. She does not know this touchy, defiant, sulky, weepy teenager anymore and she feels the loss. She senses that her daughter does not know herself either and is afraid for her as she battles through the morass of adolescence.

However, no matter what the healthy, normal adolescent girl says about Mom, no matter how much she puts her down to her friends, the mother–daughter bond offers her comfort and safety and love—if that love is secure and giving and not entangled with secret needs. Even as the teenager is beginning to gain a realistic picture of her parents and to distinguish between her values and theirs, she will continue to turn to her mother first with problems, with confidences, with questions, with doubts.

All the teenager knows is that she is changing—physically, emotionally, socially, intellectually—and that the finished person is not yet apparent. She fights with her mother to gain confirmation that she is different. In order to believe that she is no longer a child, that her new adult self is real, she needs her mother to recognize it as so. She wants her inner changes to be noticed; she wants to test her sense of what is happening against the reactions of others. She wants acknowledgment of what she feels. The problem is that her feelings change from day to day.

The mother is taken aback. She knows something important is happening to her daughter—after all, it happened to her once, too. She sees the changes, but she worries that her daughter is not ready for the journey on which she has embarked, and she is hurt when her daughter so easily dismisses her advice and expresses contempt. So she fights back. Tears flow. Doors slam. The next day, all is forgiven.

## The Healthy Mother–Daughter Bond

The process of combat is necessary and helpful to achieving the daughter's independent identity. The mother is defining the world's reaction to her child; the daughter is gauging how far she can go. She tests out her strengths, questions her behavior as well as that of others, establishes her own values and ideals. She comes to know her needs and learns to handle conflicting ones. She discovers when to compromise with the world and when to defy it. This kind of battling cannot be done internally. It needs a backboard against which to bounce.

It is a tribute to the love and strength of the relationship that the daughter turns to the mother for this purpose. It is a tribute to the mother's value and sense of herself that she does not give in to the daughter's every whim. Both learn to battle and attack and defend and end up surprising themselves with their capabilities and resources. Despite their skirmishes, the love between them is not shaken; they find some compromise so the connection is not lost forever. It is a tribute to the daughter's view of the mother that she is unafraid to attack, that she does not see her mother as fragile. She is trying to change the relationship—not end it.

When the daughter sees her mother as strong—when she understands that the basis of their relationship is unbreakable—she can feel safe within it. She can assume roles and drop them without fearing humiliation. She can test out her rage, defy and find out what it gets her, challenge without fear that she will lose what she has.

Healthy mothers and daughters, even if they look back on the turmoil with dismay, acknowledge that something important and loving was happening. It is the thirty-year-old woman who is still going through this process who needs to question what is occurring. And, even more, it is the daughter who was not allowed to experience this at any time—and still hasn't at thirty—who needs to take a good look at what she has lost.

## The Smother Mother and the Early Teen

The Smother Mother prohibits this growth. She raises you to believe that it is you two against the world. She is a fearful person who has failed to gain a solid sense of self so she tries to prevent you from doing what she has been afraid to do on her own. She is hostile and hesitant with others and complains that she has no friends.

If this is the case and you also suffer from isolating yourself from the world, you need to learn to connect with people differently and to make alliances that will support you. Initially, this may be difficult and scary. But as you let others into your life, saying and doing what comes from your heart, you will get stronger and be less afraid. Then, you might be able to serve as an example for your mother.

"When I was in high school," says Molly, now twenty-five, "if I went to a friend's house, I'd call my mom when I got there. If we'd go to the mall, I'd call her when we left. I'd call her when we got back. I told her everything because there wasn't anything bad in my life to tell.

"Then, in high school, I got into a car accident. The truth is my whole crowd was drunk and we shouldn't

have been driving, and I will never forgive myself for
what I did to my mom because my father had a problem
with alcohol, so she was fearful about me. In the emergency room, she pulled herself together and was able to
deal with it. But that whole summer vacation was spent
trying to restart talking to each other. I was so miserable
I couldn't even enjoy my friends. I felt guilty every time
I went out. Now I see that instead of putting it on the
table and saying, 'I drank too much that night. We
shouldn't have been driving. I'm not an alcoholic,
Mother. Don't worry about that. I know Dad has hurt
you and you think I'm doing that, too,' I brushed it aside
and maybe that is where my guilt came from. She kept
thinking that I was going to do it all over again, so the
whole summer was me proving to her that I was not an
evil child."

Growing up with a Smother Mother does not give you
the security you need to face yourself—or her. Real feelings
are driven into the shadows. With a mother like this, how
can you go through the experience of adolescent conflict so
necessary to defining yourself? It is only by understanding
that you are no longer the child desperate for her love that
you can begin to handle those feelings instead of seeing
them as overwhelming.

### When Hostility Has Been Smothered

When the battles that you needed to have with your mother
at fifteen were not allowed to happen, they don't go away.
All the anger that has been dismissed and repressed
explodes in your twenties and thirties but, by this time, it is
no longer healthy and productive. It is not leading you to
independence and a newfound sense of self. Typically, by

this time, the two of you are going in circles, each conflict ending with guilt and remorse and burying you more deeply in the quagmire.

It is ironic that a relationship built on the Smother Mother's refusal to acknowledge any sign of hostility turns, in the daughter's adulthood, into a battleground of continual squabbles. The mother and daughter are so chained together by unexamined fears that the tension can only be released by perpetual bickering. But these senseless battles lead only to an increase of fears.

Why does this happen? Because the Smother Mother has never encouraged her daughter to define herself outside of the role of child and the daughter has allowed herself to be seduced into remaining one. The Smother Mother may have found nursing so gratifying that she did not wean her baby until long after it was appropriate to do so. Perhaps she slept in the same bed as her little girl because it made her feel comforted and safe. As the years pass, she grows jealous and hostile toward others who want to enjoy her child and fosters the little girl's dependency on her—and her alone. She turns into a worrier and exaggerates the dangers of the outside world.

"Once, only once, I got a speeding ticket," says Elaine, thirty-six. "I came home and said, 'Ugh! I got pulled over,' and for two weeks, I heard about it. Every time I left, it was, 'Don't step on the gas. Watch yourself. Be careful!'

"In my house, the message was always, 'Don't venture out. It's scary out there. What if I need you? Stay within reach, just in case.' *Just in case* was never specified. All her life, she has done the three things she's always done: she goes to work, comes home, makes dinner for my father. She's timid and rejecting of new ideas, nervous, and picky. When she comes to visit me, she tries to help but she'll say, 'I don't know where to put these dishes. Someone else is going to have to put them away. I didn't empty the dish tray because I couldn't figure out where everything went.'

"Once, when I was a kid, there was a light snow and I planned on going to school anyway and she stood in the hall and wept, 'You'll be the only person in the building. There will be nobody else there but you. You are going to be outside alone and everybody is going to think you're an orphan!' I was scared to death so I stayed home."

## When Rebellion Has Been Smothered

In threatening to run away and then not leaving, in cursing her mother and then taking it back, in dumping all her frustration on her mother and then finding herself forgiven, in criticizing her mother and then changing her mind—the healthy teenager truly learns something about love between mother and daughter. This young woman does not live in terror of losing her mother; she does not anticipate abandonment or disaster at every turn. This daughter will grow up with a strong sense of her powers, feelings of independence and competence, and the knowledge that she can survive separation because she knows that her mother loves her, respects her, hears her—and will always be there for her.

The daughter of the Smother Mother, on the other hand, has had little experience with rebellion so she lives with the expectation that, should she act on such a desire, it will result in rejection by her mother and spending the rest of her days isolated and alone. Never having tested life for fear of the loss of her mother's love, she lives in fear of abandonment. She has never gone through the mother–daughter conflict so necessary to finding her own identity. She has little knowledge of the inevitability of forgiveness in a loving relationship. The healthy adolescent girl grows into womanhood with a solid trust in her mother's love; the crippled daughter needs it all the more because their relationship seems so tenuous.

On some level, the daughter of the Smother Mother is aware that her mother has not been responding to her, that the smothering is a way of denying her—not hearing her, not loving her. Even a tot knows when a smile is inappropriate, when she is being overpraised, when she is found to be cute though she meant to be serious. This lack of honest responsiveness on the mother's part is a way of ignoring the real child, which is why her love has never been trusted and why the daughter believes it can always be withdrawn.

## What's in Store for the Smother Mother's Daughter?

The daughter of the Smother Mother often turns into an obedient, "good" girl. Typically, she is a top-notch student, gets good grades, is accepted into good schools, and is rewarded for being "mature." She excels in any situation where the expectations are defined by others.

> Caroline graduated at the top of her law school class, got a job working for a criminal attorney, and ended up spending decades doing the legwork—writing up briefs, preparing strategies, laying the groundwork for cases— so that her boss could go into court, get the glory, be on T.V., and raise his fees astronomically. The more powerful he became, the more Caroline feared that if she demanded more—more money, a chance to try a case herself, some acknowledgment—he could get another

smart graduate to take over her position. Well into her thirties, she found herself at a career dead end, feeling that she had no power of her own. What had happened to her brilliant potential?

Caroline was the daughter of a Smother Mother and, in denying her forbidden feelings, she had also inhibited a major part of her personality. She had buried not only her anger but also aggression, assertiveness, and ambition. It is difficult to distinguish between anger and assertiveness. You can learn how only if you are allowed to test and explore your feelings.

Because Caroline never had the opportunity to find her own voice, as a grown woman she stepped effortlessly into the role of the backup. It wasn't that she felt deprived of her just rewards; in fact, it never occurred to her to ask for any of the perks due to her as the firm expanded. She simply assumed her boss would grant her these when they were due and, in fact, she was always more comfortable in the background.

"It's safe to be anonymous," Caroline says about her life, "dangerous to be visible." She will stand in line at the supermarket checkout and, if someone pushes in before her, she never makes a fuss. She does not question authority. To be angry causes disruption. It is not that she fights the impulse; the impulse is numbed. So, for years, she has stayed at her job, never acknowledging how unhappy she is, how deprived she feels, how unfairly she is being treated.

She lives at home with her mother but her fear of conflict, her desire to be a good girl, and her difficulty knowing what she truly wants are nearly paralyzing. Her mother prepares all the meals and, if Caroline wants a light dinner and her mother has prepared steak, Caroline obediently eats the steak.

"This is so silly," she says, near tears. As she talks, she loses control and begins to shock herself with what she is saying. "But the one thing that used to annoy me was when Mom and I would go for a walk on a summer evening. We would stop at the local Ben and Jerry's and I would order a cone. Mom would always refuse to buy one. She would say she'd take a taste of mine instead. I used to rage in my head, 'Can't she have one of her own?' But my reaction seemed so stupid, so exaggerated. I couldn't imagine saying it so it went on, night after night, year after year, and I learned to live with it."

### Turning into Mom

A young woman who has been deprived of an open, free-wheeling, combative, expressive relationship with a loving mother may feel flawed and incomplete and suffer from feelings of emptiness—always sensing that she's missing something, but never able to define it and certainly not able to ask for it. Worse, she finds herself following her mother's path. She has incorporated her mother's sense of the world so thoroughly into her life that she cannot tell where she ends and her mother begins.

"I am my mother," says Bridget, twenty-one, "and I don't like it. She was eighteen and living in a small town when she met my father and moved to L.A. She worshipped the ground he walked on. In the end, it was the cause of their divorce but she continues to be dependent on a man in relationship after relationship. I didn't date in high school and now, for the first time, I'm involved with a guy, Greg, and am putting all my friends aside. I run after him and that's all I seem to do. I thought I had developed into a pretty independent person. I moved away from home and was pleased with what was going on but I've been in a rut for four months. I'm happy because I care about someone but the rest of my life is gone.

"Mom loves it. The first thing she asks when she calls is, 'How's Greg?' I was home for two weeks and he came to visit and she said, 'You'd better get a haircut before he comes.' Then it was, 'What are you going to wear this weekend?'

"I was ecstatic when I first moved away, full of so many ideas of what I wanted to do. I need to finish college—I have three semesters left—and I should be doing that. My goal is to get an accounting degree and then my C.P.A. I want to be my own boss but I'm not doing it. I was out of work for three months; basically I stopped working when I met Greg. He was opening a new store and asked if I could help him set up a computer accounting system so I spent all my time doing that.

"My mom kept saying, 'You should be out looking for a job. Stop going to the store.' I got a job and my Mom came up two weeks ago. The store was busy when we dropped by so she said, 'Why don't you see to that customer over there?' First she thought my helping him was a bad thing, now she thinks I should because that would make him happy.

"I guess my mom is a very giving person but, if you give away too much of yourself, you are nothing but a shell. But I'm afraid if I change he might get upset and not feel about me the way he does now. Yesterday, I told him I couldn't come over because I had plans and he said, 'If you're going to choose your friends over me, we're going to have a big problem.'

" 'I've chosen you over my friends for the last four months,' I answered. 'They are my family here.' In the end, he said that I was right—but I had taken a chance and was afraid he might leave. It was a little step for me but an important one. The next step is to see if I can go to school and pursue my goals at the same time as I have a relationship. Because if I don't, I'll fall into every pattern my mother has fallen into and that scares the living daylights out of me."

## Separation: The Freedom to Differ

Even healthy mothers and daughters have trouble with the complicated process of separation, but the problems increase when your mother depends on you to fill unspoken needs and expects you to share her deepest fears.

Separation is not loss; it is not cutting yourself off from someone you love. Rather, it creates a space so that two equal, authentic beings can relate to one another. Separation does not mean that you have to stand alone and have no wants or needs. No one wants to be all alone and unable to relate in a loving way. Women need their mothers and want to love them.

However, separation does mean that you are free to differ. If your mother's favorite color is blue, your favorite color does not have to be blue. Loving exists even when there are differences. The healthy adolescent girl shouts at her mother, "I don't want to be exactly like you. I want to live my own life!" The secure mother responds, "I am not asking you to be like me. I know you are different from me." If you have never experienced that moment with your mother, you have not yet found the freedom to be yourself.

> Terry, forty-three, and her mother were having one of their perpetual squabbles, this time over the fact that Terry hadn't hung curtains in her apartment. Terry brushed Mom off by saying she hadn't had time but the nagging persisted.
>
> "The truth is," Terry confesses, "that I hate curtains because she used to take them down, wash them, and change them three times a year. The ritual drove me crazy!"
>
> Terry did not want this spat to build, as they usually did, to a knockdown, drag-out battle, with tears, insults, and phone calls to relatives with opposing accusations. So she tried to stay calm and said to her mother between gritted teeth, "Ma, there is one thing you've got to understand. I'm me and you're you!"
>
> Her mother looked as though her daughter were speaking in tongues. Terry pointed a trembling finger to the ground and drew an imaginary line between them.
>
> "You get it, Ma? We are not the same. I'm me and you're you!"
>
> Her mother thought it over, then shrugged.
>
> "Yeah," she sighed, "but what difference does it make?"

It does make a difference. You seeing your mother as who she is, her seeing you as who you are, and both of you respecting that imaginary line on the ground.

"Daughters of neurotic mothers must try to separate," says New York City psychotherapist Roberta Schultz. "If you are still living at home and can't do it physically, you must do it emotionally. If you can't do it with your heart, try to do it with your head. The best way to cope is to see what your mother is doing, even though she will never see, and remove yourself by not getting engaged with her in whatever the pattern."

If you are under the thumb of the Smother Mother, the price you are paying may not be immediately clear to you. She has so much power that you dare not feel your lack of independence, the deprivations. Instead, you will experience these in your love life, in your career, and in your feelings about yourself. It is safer to numb your impulses than to criticize her, which makes it doubly difficult for you to escape.

Before you can think of a solution, before you can analyze the problem, you must make sure you are thinking *your* thoughts, not Mom's. This can be difficult if you have never done it before, if you have incorporated her sense of the world so thoroughly into your life that you cannot tell the difference any more.

What do you do? Understand that you are facing a tough task, that you are at last trying to do what should have been done in gradual steps all your life, bit by bit, and you can start the process of separating.

First, find some physical space to call your own, which will provide some sense of privacy in your life. If it is at all possible to leave home, do so. The move will fill you with guilt and apprehension and, once you have made it, things won't be easy—but you'll never be able to sort through your relationship with your mother while you allow her to hover over your every move.

If it is impossible to leave home, establish some limits on her intrusions. If she listens in on your phone conversations, get your own phone line. If she goes through your mail, rent a post office box. Insist that she is not allowed to go through your possessions and that she may not enter your room without knocking. These kinds of basic limits are usually established by adolescents. These simple demands for human dignity are ones that you can and should make—without doubting their validity, without giving in to guilt.

This does not mean that you won't feel anxiety or remorse—you will. When you are stepping into uncharted territory, when you are threatening the familiar structure of your life (and hers), you must expect that she will object, get insulted, even accuse you of treachery. She may weep and claim you are hurting her beyond belief. You may believe her, waiver, feel anxious. Your impulse will be to rush to her and beg forgiveness. Don't. The anxiety will pass. Only then will you get a glimmer of how much you have sacrificed to fears for so many years. Only then will the buried parts of yourself begin to flicker with life. Only then will some clarity emerge in your thinking.

You can learn to deal with anxiety simply by experiencing it. Living with anxiety is the only way you can start to acknowledge the deadened parts in yourself. Remember that it is no longer Mom doing the damage; whole areas of your personality and impulses are not functioning. In the process of awakening them, there will be tension, regrets, guilt. But you must dig past these feelings in order to bring what has been buried to life.

The first time that you set limits on your mother's smothering behavior and can feel justified and good about it, you will get a sense of the kind of power that has been denied you. If you have spent your life calling her every day, not because you wanted to, but because you felt obligated to, tell her that you are too busy these days and promise to call on the weekends. This is a perfectly reasonable compromise for a grown woman to offer her mother. If she threatens that she could be dying and nobody would know, stick to your guns. Test your own reactions. The more you suffer after setting such a simple limit, the more you know you have a serious problem that needs to be addressed!

Once you have found your own physical space—your own apartment, your own telephone line, a locked diary—you can begin to explore what is going on intellectually. You cannot expect to change a pattern of deeply embedded feelings and reactions overnight, but you can begin to think about what you are feeling, understand where the feelings are coming from, and start to explore the reasonableness of your reactions. That is the first step in changing your feelings.

## Strategies for Change

- This is your life you are trying to reclaim! Each tiny triumph will give you the courage to go for another. Like every other achievement in life, separating from your mother takes practice. If you were not given the opportunity to learn as a child, be patient with yourself as an adult. After each small success, you'll feel less fear as you try for the next. While it may seem impossible when you are locked in the past, things do get easier.
- Stop wrangling with your mother over insignificant things. Stop trying to win arguments. You are only trapping yourself in your old ways of relating, sinking deeper and deeper into the entanglement, where you end up feeling guilty, angry, or misunderstood. In order to start working on *yourself,* you need to free yourself from your dependence on your mother. There was a time when she was vital to your survival, but that time is past. When you can avoid being drawn into a never-ending cycle, you are free to form better relations with other people and your mother's influence becomes less important.

- Wait until it's a done deed before you tell your mother. One young woman whose smothering mother is a Worrier offers this advice: "I've learned not to tell her about things that are in process. I wait until after it's done. I don't talk to her about my job right now because I may move to a different department and instantly she'd go, 'Well, is that good for you?' or 'Are you making the right decision?' and that's stressful for me. We have said things in the past that were hurtful so I try not to let it get to that point.

  "We had one fight where she actually broke down the door to rip the phone out of my wall. So now I tend to talk about light things. I sit down and am quiet and let her talk. I think about her and why she acts the way she does and almost want to protect her because she is getting older and becoming vulnerable and things are happening in her life. I feel happy that I have finally reached a point where I don't say something just to hurt her. We can talk about the dungarees she wants to buy at the store, things that aren't serious, and I tend to be more sympathetic when she gets the way she does, which makes it easier between us."

- Instead of battling with her, take a walk. Give yourself a moment to review what went on. Attempt to differentiate your reactions from Mom's and, even if they embarrass you, even if you have been brought up to think that what you are feeling is wrong, respect your feelings because they are a part of you. Developing greater tolerance for your feelings can heal and promote growth, in and of itself. Self-acceptance permits you to discard denial and to increase trust in your own judgment and sense of reality.

- If you are unable to stop an argument over some unimportant detail, try to analyze it after the fact. You'll gain a better understanding of what happened. Your behavior will begin to separate from your mother's as a result of this understanding. This is the intellectual aspect of separation; however, do not expect immediate emotional freedom, which might take years to accomplish. The same ground has to be fought for time and again, the same victories have to be achieved over and over. Women fighting to separate from their smothering mothers and to find their own voice sometimes say that they never truly get over the emotional costs, the guilt, the pain. But if you can step off the merry-go-round, you can, at least, breathe.

# 5

# The Merger Mom
## *The Late Teen Sets Boundaries*

*S*helley, twenty-seven years old and a law school student, is currently working as a paralegal. She is tall, voluptuous, and perhaps overweight, but she carries it with confidence.

"If I could be thirty or forty pounds thinner," she says, "my mother would be the happiest person in the world. Her day consists of waking up, running from home to the gym, two hours in the gym, coming home to change, and playing tennis and then golf. She's always pushing me to go to exercise class and, when I used to live with my parents, I would come home before she arrived, put gym clothes on, mess my hair, throw my sneakers in the middle of the room and take a nap. Even when I was away at school, I would lie to her and say, 'Oh, I just came from the gym,' or she would ask, 'Are you going to the gym?' If I said no, she'd say, 'So when are you going to get back into it?'

"I'd say, 'When I have time I'll get back into it.' And she'd say, 'I don't understand why you don't have time to get back into it now.'

"If I'd had enough courage, I would have said, 'You know what? Why don't I step away from my life for a while and you can live it exactly the way you want me to live it and then I can do what I want to do!'"

Shelley has a deep throaty laugh, which is heard often—she's a tough New Yorker with a sharp sense of humor. She looks every bit the independent, courageous, successful, modern woman—but is she?

"I live ten blocks from my parents so my mother stops by a lot. She drops things off for me. She has a key in case she needs to make phone calls when she is in the neighborhood. I don't like it but my parents pay half the rent so I really can't say anything. While I was at work one day she wanted to show a friend of hers my apartment so that they could compare it with the friend's daughter's and then she called me to say my apartment was a mess. I said, 'If I'd known you were coming, I would have cleaned.' But I don't get angry with her. I take it out in other ways—like I won't clean my apartment. She'll notice there's dust on the back of my couch. She walks to the kitchen, takes a wet rag, and starts cleaning. Then she'll hire a housekeeper for me. What the hell. If she's gonna pay, I don't say a word.

"In high school, she used to write my papers. When I applied to college, she wrote my personal essay. All I had to do was sign the applications. While I was away at school, she managed to phone me every day. If I wasn't in my apartment, she would get the number of wherever I was from my roommate and then call me there.

"In my senior year, I had to pick a career. 'Why don't you be a teacher?' she said. 'You'll have summers off, that's a perfect career. Apply to graduate school and be a teacher, okay?' 'Okay,' I said.

"I applied to graduate school and got a job as an assistant teacher. I was the most miserable human being alive. There was not a ray of anything in life to enjoy. I hated teaching; I had just graduated and here I was back in school, living with them, crying every night. I dropped out of graduate school and just drifted about and it took me five years to apply for law school with a lot of coaxing and support—but not from them!

"I'm in therapy now. She actually precipitated my going because she was concerned that I didn't have men coming to Thanksgiving dinner and she always said that I don't flirt well. She felt she had to know when I was going on dates and then she'd say, 'Why didn't he call again? Were you not nice to him? What did you wear? Did you wear ripped jeans?' I'm not allowed to wear ripped jeans in front of her. 'When they call do you not make plans? I don't understand why you're so non-committal. Were you rude to him on the phone?'

"The first time I walked into therapy, I sat down and said that I have a wonderful family, a terrific mother, everything is fine. I wanted to focus on the funk I seemed to be in and three months later it came out that I have this problem: I needed to talk to my mother every single day—from the street corner I would call her! She needs to know everything that's going on and these phone calls were driving me crazy.

"My therapist said the first thing I had to do was to stop telling her everything. My reaction was, 'No way! Are you kidding?' and, when I complained, he would say, 'Why did you tell her that?' and I would respond, 'I thought I had to. She needs to hear it.'

"The truth is that I didn't have to tell her everything. Now she never knows when I go out on dates. It drives her insane. I hear it in her voice when we talk on the phone. I find myself lying and feel guilty, but it's come to a point where she has to back off. She is literally stunting my growth. I'm twenty-seven years old and she is still judging the way I dress, the way I look.

"Getting into law school without my parents having anything to do with it allowed me to finally believe in myself. I just finished my very first paper and my mother doesn't know what it's on. That's a big step. This is my way of saying, 'I'm going to be a damned good lawyer and you'll have nothing to do with it.' And I love my job. But she still doesn't get it. The other day, she called at 9 A.M. to find out if I wanted to go shopping with her. 'You don't have to go to work today, do you? Because it's too cold to play golf and I thought maybe you wanted to go shopping with me.' When I told her no, that I had to be at work, she said, 'I just figured you could go in around one. I didn't think it would be a problem because I'd take you up to Donna Karan.'

"If you had sat me down a year and a half ago and asked me to tell you about me and my mother, I would have told you we are so close that we talk every day, she knows everything about me, and I know everything about her. Now I realize we were not close. I go to her for approval, but she doesn't know much about me and I know very little about her. I couldn't tell you her favorite color or her favorite food. All we talked about was how my friends are doing.

"I grew up very privileged. My parents went away every weekend and these phone calls would come, 'How are you doing? There's money in the dish. The driver is outside to take you wherever you need to go.' As advantaged as we were, we were neglected. I think now I always wanted her love and approval, so maybe I didn't feel as loved as I thought. I figured out early that the more I could tell her, the more she would love me. I could measure her love by how long I could keep her on the phone. Yet there was no quality or substance to our conversation because she was so self-absorbed.

"Four years ago I wanted to be just like her. I wasn't ready to see what she'd done to me, how she'd ripped me apart and criticized me and put me in this position of such low self-confidence that I had no idea who I was. She's a nice person, everybody loves her, but it's been tough being her daughter. Now I need to move beyond the difficulty and make it an easy thing to be myself.

"I can't say I don't miss the way it was, the ease of our relationship. Now I feel I have to combat her because I am trying to change something. One of the most fulfilling feelings is that I am not alone—there are so many people out there going through the exact same thing. I am not the only woman with a mother who has ripped me to shreds."

By this point, her easy laughter has vanished and Shelley looks different—maybe more serious, maybe less happy—a person struggling to be whole.

# Qualities of the Merger Mom

The Merger Mom absorbs you. She wants to own you and needs to know every detail of your life. The Merger Mom does not allow the infant to comfort herself in the crib and fall asleep on her own but rushes to pick up the baby at the first sign of discomfort. She proclaims it as a sign of her sensitivity and compassion and is unable to see that the child will not learn to soothe herself this way. Step by step, through childhood, she does not allow her daughter to do things on her own, to rely on herself and develop creative problem-solving abilities. In fact, the little girl gets the message that any desire for independence, for experimentation, for space for herself will create dismay and disapproval.

The child of a Merger Mom is not being loved, she is being absorbed. She is not being heard, she is being muffled. Growing up without a sense of boundaries, privacy, or respect for the self, she feels less of a person, not more. She feels more scared, not less. Very often, along with her taste in clothes, her views, and her values in life, the Merger Mom insists that her daughter take on her fears and that she take on her daughter's.

"I got a staph infection in my face last year," says twenty-year-old Robin. "The plastic surgeon had to cut quickly because it was a matter of getting my face open and getting the infection out, and my mom felt like she should have asked questions or gotten a second opinion or stopped him. For a week, she slept on the floor next to my hospital bed. Now, I don't even see the scar. I'm happy that I'm healthy and safe but my mom got very irrational. My dad told me she tried to cut her own face because she was so upset, because she loves me so much.

"As a result, every day after work I feel obligated to stop by at home and let her know that I'm okay. It's made everything more difficult to deal with."

## What's Behind Mom's Behavior?

You should be able to say, "I'm scared. I'm lonely. Help me out of this mess," and your mother should reassure you, offer comfort, help you to find the courage to go on. The Merger Mom doubles your fears. This mother has a craving to be totally connected with her daughter because of her own sense of incompleteness. She is unable to stand on her own and contains her anxiety by living through her daughter. She feels powerful in relation to this child the way she does not in relation to her life.

The daughter becomes an extension of the mother—a chance to "do it over" and get the gratification denied her in her own childhood and current life. The Merger Mother needs to be needed. If needed, she feels important and your dependency helps her to overlook the gaping holes in her own life.

There seem to be many advantages. The Merger Mom is always there for you. She usually lives nearby and is available in any emergency. She helps you out financially. She buys you clothes. She gives you advice and seems to know more than you do. She offers constant support as long as you don't cross her—and daughters of Merger Moms learn not to do that early on.

Her behavior might be presented as overpowering love and you accept it as that. But where there is no recognition of the other person as "other" there is no real love.

## The Healthy Mom and the Late Teen

There is a difference between connecting and merging. Wanting to connect is a vital part of being human and we all have moments when we need to be taken care of—even as teenagers. An intimate relationship with your mom is one of the great joys in life. In a good relationship, you respect each other's individuality, give one another space, nourish each other's goals, and support each other's struggles. You connect—but you are not one.

The healthy mother will feel pride as her daughter hurdles new obstacles—obstacles that the mother herself might never have dared to tackle. Every mother grieves the loss of her importance to her daughter's life. But if there has been honesty and respect all along, they will be able to negotiate the transitions in life: the daughter's first day of school or her first date or her success in a new sport. These experiences help them adjust later on to the daughter's marriage or her setting out on a career or becoming a mother in her own right. As both women grow and change, their relationship will be marked by cooperation, friendship, and some role reversal, especially as the mother ages and faces losses or illness. The daughter of a healthy mother will be able to offer her mother love and support without resentment.

## The Merger Mom and the Late Teen

"I was in love with a boy for four and a half years in high school," says Michelle, nineteen. "Although my mom had always sworn to raise me differently than her mom raised her—she wanted me to go out for sports and take science classes and math and things like that—the minute I met Richie she was busy buying me clothes so that I looked good when I went out with him.

"Just a couple of years ago, my dad finally learned how to boil water and make rice. If you asked my mom, she would say that one of the worst things she ever did was cater to him when they were first married, but she encouraged me to focus on Richie and I took to it like it was second nature. I never stopped playing my flute, was still on the swim team, and still got straight As, but those things became hard to concentrate on.

"In the four and a half years we dated, I missed only one of Richie's football games—and my mom went for me. After we broke up, she sat on the bed and cried with me because she felt betrayed by him also. She had been so proud of him. He was very tall and she loved it, she said, when he put his arm around her and they walked around the football field.

"But she didn't say anything to comfort me—like 'It's okay, you'll get over it.' Instead, she said, 'Well, you tend to push people away.' It was then that I began to wonder what was going on."

## Sexuality

The merged mother–daughter relationship might work until the daughter begins developing sexually. Sex is private, sex is personal, sex cannot be shared with the mother—and certainly not the Merger Mom to whom anything private in her daughter's life represents the loss of her own identity. She pretends to approve, pushing the daughter toward a boy she can control. She likes the boys who could not possibly excite the girl. The daughter of the Merger Mom has two options: either she can remain attached to her mother by burying her sexuality or she can use it as her area of rebellion and escape.

Healthy development of your sexuality requires a sense of boundaries. You cannot enjoy a loss of control until you are safe in the knowledge that you can regain it. You can't share your feelings and your body with another if you are afraid of invasion. On the other hand, if you dive into sex without a sense of self, you tend to do what you have always done: look to fulfill others' desires, fail to take responsibility for your own needs, find men to merge with, and continue denying yourself.

With little practice in seeing herself as an adult, the daughter of a Merger Mom may behave irresponsibly about contraception. She depends on the man to take care of her. She avoids any discussion of birth control or dealing with the consequences of sex without birth control. In this way, she steps into chronological adulthood while remaining a little girl. She ends up, once again, dependent.

## What Are Boundaries?

The Merger Mom connects without any respect for boundaries—borders that define territories, physical as well as emotional. As adults, we don't want our mothers leaning over in public and brushing our hair from our eyes. This would be demeaning and invasive. We need to feel a sense of privacy, of control over our bodies as well as our feelings. We must have private spaces, physically and emotionally, where we can evaluate our aims, our values, our sense of ourselves despite the opinions of others. In all relationships, it is essential for us to have a secure place to go in which to replenish our needs.

Boundaries protect. If they are not respected, you live in fear of invasion and put up defensive walls. Without boundaries, you find yourself permitted only to feel what your mother is feeling, just as she insists on feeling what you do. If she is sad, you are sad. If you are happy and she is sad, you learn to suppress your happy feelings. If your tears so overwhelm her with grief that you end up burdened by guilt, you learn to present a perpetually cheerful front. If she thinks you are wrong—you think so too. You respond to the outside world the way she would. You judge your behavior the way she would. You look to Mom for protection, yet the Merger Mom responds by reinforcing the danger. Your life and hers become merged.

If you have not been trained to establish boundaries with your mother, you'll have difficulty doing so with friends, your husband, and your children. You'll be overwhelmed by the needs of others and never acknowledge what you are after.

Establishing boundaries involves defining what you will give to your mother as well as what you will take from her. For example, you cannot accept money and give nothing in return. You can't set boundaries that say only "keep out." You must let her know where she will be included. This means that you have to decide what is imperative for you to control and what part of your life you are willing to share.

It is important to recognize what is behind your mother's behavior so that your self-assertion does not become a continuation of the power struggle. You also need to acknowledge the part of you that wants to keep things the way they are and your conflicting feelings of loss, sadness, and helplessness—without giving in to them.

Setting boundaries allows you to take your first steps into true adulthood—a state that may frighten you.

## What's in Store for the Merger Mom's Daughter?

Often, this young woman settles into Mom's orbit for her entire life. She sees herself as just like her mother. She proclaims to all how much she loves her mom, what a great mother she is, and how lost she would be without her. She trumpets the similarities in their lives. She marries—after all, Mom did—but the connection with her husband dare not threaten the connection with her mother. Many times, the daughter's husband is treated as an intruder in the family or as a necessary stud to deliver grandchildren to Mom.

The daughter needs the mother as much as the mother needs the daughter. In fact, all the neighbors beam at such a strong mother–daughter connection. Other women envy the mom whose daughter calls her three times a day. Nobody wants to look beneath the surface.

With no alternative but to repeat her mother's life, the young woman is confined within the limits her mother has set for herself. But why would a young woman want to turn her back on everything the modern world offers to live the same life as her mother did? Because, to the daughter of the Merger Mom, to want more than her mother had, to become more than she did, might cause a rift, might mean she will lose her.

The daughter of the Merger Mom has a fear of independence, of individuality. She refuses to stand out and as a result tends to be a low achiever. She fears experimentation, keeps her problems a secret, and boasts about her limited life. She does not see that the quality of love that she was brought up with has created a trap.

This love from the Merger Mom is offered only to the little girl in you. So you keep needing more of it. You crave the merging as much as she does. And you pass on this tangled concept of love to your husband and daughters.

## Rebellion Without Boundaries

"I was a little adult all my life," says Rona, twenty-nine. "Home at midnight like I was supposed to. If for any reason I couldn't, I'd call and tell them I'd be late. Then, at seventeen I got involved with a crazy guy who lived by no rules whatsoever. That was a major rebellion. Pretty soon, I got pregnant so we married and moved in with my folks. Before I knew it, I was pregnant again. At nineteen, I looked around and thought, 'Boy, if that was rebellion, did you goof!' "

The daughter of the Merger Mom rebels by staying out late, slamming doors, and getting involved with men she cannot take home to Mom. She may behave as if she is not afraid of anything but, if she goes to bed with a man and he doesn't call afterwards, she suffers terrible humiliation. Without a sense of boundaries, it is hard for her to pull herself together after an invasion.

"I started rebelling early," says Didi, now in her forties. "My most vivid childhood memory is of having a girl-friend pick me up in the eighth grade and my mother was insisting that I wear a sweater. I can still hear her screaming, humiliating me. She couldn't even let me make my own decision about that sweater. That's when I started keeping secrets. I stole from her. I slept over at girlfriends' houses as often as I could. At fourteen, I was running off to college frat-house parties. By the time I was seventeen, I was into drugs; it started with pot, then acid, then anything, and I ran away to California.

"I'd do anything to get away from her. I got married, had a kid, got unmarried. We lived in a commune and I was able to share being a mother with all these other young mothers. All I ever wanted was to belong. My second husband was a drug dealer. In all those years, I never once was involved with a guy who got up in the morning and went to work. My daughter went to twelve different schools in her first few years, we never lived anyplace long.

"Then I got involved in an abusive affair that lasted seven years. In all this time, my parents must have thought I was gay because I never talked about men. There was always a man in my life but they never knew any of them. I was living my life designed to keep my mother away."

Independence implies standing up for yourself. Being against something is only half of the equation. If you knock down the walls to freedom but cannot step through and claim it, you have rebelled but are not free. If you are thrilled with your behavior only because it is something of which your mother would disapprove, you are not enjoying the present—you are still tied to the past.

If you are in your late twenties and are not living responsibly, not paying your bills, not showing up for work, having a lot of sex without really enjoying it, and relishing experiences only in proportion to how shocked your mother would be if she knew, you are stuck in adolescence. You know what you want to say "no" to but there is no "yes" in your life.

Rebellion may be required in order to get your mother to listen to you, to gain control over some space in which you can figure things out. But then you have to define yourself as something other than a reaction to her. Once you recognize that becoming the opposite of your mother is not necessarily becoming yourself, you have taken a step to finding fulfillment.

## Merged for a Lifetime

Many mothers and daughters remain merged for a lifetime but their relationship is sustained only with a great deal of self-deception.

> Valerie, thirty-four, is the mother of two and currently going through a divorce, yet she has the ambience and manner of a child. She giggles a lot, talks in a little-girl voice, has no real confidence in her own opinions, and says one thing, then changes her mind and giggles.
>
> "When I was six or seven, I classified my mother as 'cool.' I remember us sitting on a blanket at park concerts and she had on a headband and a minidress. She was outspoken on political issues, involved in campaigns, handed out leaflets on the corner, and, whatever stand she took, we had to share her position. I couldn't have a Barbie doll because she didn't want me to grow up believing that Barbie was the 'perfect' woman—but, when you're a child, if you want a Barbie doll, you want a Barbie.
>
> "I have a very close relationship with her but she still controls every aspect of my life. If I have a free weekend,

she'll say, 'Why don't you come here and sleep over and eat dinner and we'll do everything?' and I have a hard time getting her to understand I have to go food shopping and do my laundry.

"She's a sociologist, published in her field, a college professor, and I rebelled by getting married when I was nineteen instead of finishing school. Then she said, 'Don't have children,' so by the time I was twenty-three, I had two children. She hated my husband. She wanted me to marry someone stable, a professional, someone in my class and I married out of my class, an Italian from a very poor family.

"She says you couldn't tell me anything; I think she should have stopped my marriage. She had to go to Italy to bring him over here because there were problems with immigration and, if she didn't like him that much, there must have been a way she could have stopped it. She didn't like my boyfriend here, which was why she and my dad sent me to Europe in the first place. If they could uproot me from America, it seems like she could have done something instead of allowing the marriage to take place.

"My marriage was doomed from the start. I was stupid; he was twenty-eight to my nineteen. He took advantage of a child and he was a real creep about it. After my daughter was born, he decided he didn't like me any more; this was after a year and a half. Technically, we should have stopped the marriage then and there but it lasted fourteen years. That's the way I am.

"My mother might have had a lot to do with his feelings because every weekend we'd go to her house. When I was pregnant, I'd sleep there. When my children were little, she never babysat. She'd say, 'I'd rather have you and the kids. Why should I take the kids, then I don't see you?' When my husband had a business and it wasn't succeeding, she'd tell him what to do. Because she's a sociologist she had very strong opinions about child-rearing: the baby has to sleep in the family bed because primates sleep with their mothers till they are four. Also she had a theory that infants forget to breathe if they don't hear the mother breathing and there was a correlation between that and sudden infant death syndrome. So my children slept with me.

"Now that I'm going through a divorce, she's telling the lawyer what she wants done. I guess I'm used to being controlled. I always thought she was the smartest person in the world so I'm glad to have her now because I am still under my ex-husband's thumb and she can see things I can't. She only wants what's good for me.

"I describe my family as the true extended family. The real nuclear family is my mother, my father, me, and my children. They allowed my husband a place when he was there, but I don't think my family was what my husband wanted. I know my mother will die one day and that will be the worst thing because she's my closest friend.

"We phone each other three or four times a day. When my parents are on vacation, we talk almost daily. When we don't talk, I feel lost because I have nobody to talk to. Most of the time, I take my vacations with them. When my husband and I split, I was taken to the Cape with the kids for a couple of weeks by them. Now they're in my life even more.

"I work in an after-school program Wednesdays and Thursdays and I am not allowed to let my children wait for me at home alone because Mom feels 'one day is fine, not two days.' So the children are dragged to her house on Wednesdays and she feeds them dinner, they do their homework, then I pick them up and we go home. I really don't want to take my kids to her on Wednesdays because I have to get to my job and it makes me rushed. They could go home. They could take the bus and wait for me, but I guess I'm used to doing what I'm told so I just do. It's not coercion. I just listen and I do.

"I'm not an adult. Even my mother says she doesn't see me as an adult. I see myself as half an adult, but when I want to be seen by my mom as an adult, I'm not. Last weekend, at their country house, I wanted to leave at four, not when they left, and that became an issue because she wanted me to stay longer. Luckily, my father stepped in and I was able to leave early. If he hadn't, it just would have gone on and on. Usually, I end up coerced into doing what she wants me to do.

"They're helping me out financially until our settlement kicks in. It was scary to decide to divorce, but now I feel like I was never married and I thank god it is over. I don't want to deal with him. I'd rather be alone with my kids and my apartment. Anyway, I'm not alone because I have my mother as a support system. I like my weekends alone when the kids are with my husband. But last weekend, I was with my folks at least a day.

"She's already told me I'm not allowed to have a boyfriend near my children. Okay, I can understand that but she's given me a time limit. I can't have a boyfriend for a year. I can't have anyone come to my house. I can't have my children exposed to the fact that I might have a friend because it's bad for them. Then, after a year, I can have someone just come over so they can get used to him. So I have this regimented schedule set and I go along with whatever she says unless I feel strongly about something—but I haven't felt that.

"At this point, I don't want to get involved with a guy. I don't want to be bothered. If I do meet a guy and she doesn't like him, I'll listen since I didn't listen the first time around. I'm better off not relating to anybody and she supports that. Push comes to shove, people who are not family will take what they can get and, when you're no longer of any use, that's it. I was always the perfect child and I still am, at thirty-four."

# Separation: Facing Your Fears

Valerie is kidding herself. She says that she wants to be alone, yet she never is alone. She says that she wants to be seen as an adult yet she admits that she doesn't feel like one. She blames her mother and her husband for her failed marriage. She submits to her mother's decisions about the divorce because she sees herself as under her husband's thumb. She twists and turns to maintain the comfort level of what she has known, where she feels safe.

We all do this. The greatest obstacle to emotional growth is self-deception. This is the reason you need to look at the whole picture without lies. You need to see what is going on before you are able to change it.

Separating from the Merger Mom can be more complicated than with other moms because there seem to be so many satisfactions in the arrangement. As the merged daughter, you get security, protection, and companionship. You are able to abdicate responsibility for your own life. While living within this mother–daughter bubble, you do not have to make adult choices, which reduces the anxiety in your life. Mom concentrates on your fears. You concentrate on hers. In fact, both of you are using the merger to avoid dealing with yourselves—but only by facing your fears can you change.

If Valerie gave herself the opportunity to look at the reality—to acknowledge the helplessness, the anger, and the demeaning sense of herself in her current situation— she might resolve to move out of this merged relationship. The one area in which she expressed direct unhappiness was about bringing her kids to her mother's every Wednesday. She could decide to tackle that issue and see what happens.

It is a case where there is no objective right or wrong. Her mother might be correct that it is not good for the kids to come home to an empty apartment. But Valerie is also right that the pressure to get them to her mother's before work is creating so much tension that the kids may be adversely affected. There are pros and cons to both sides of the issue and it would be feasible for Valerie to say, "Mom, you may be right about this but I may be also. So, this time, I'm going with my gut impulses and needs." She is not proposing the decision for her mother's approval. She is not opening it up for discussion. She is not even rejecting her mother's argument. She is simply stating that she has a right to make a decision based on her perceptions. What would her mother do? Abandon her?

If Valerie has thought it out in private, if she has recognized what she needs, if she approached her mother calmly, she might walk away with a piece of her life reclaimed. But she will not be able to do that if she continues "listening and doing," if she does not stop fooling herself about how satisfactory the present situation is for her.

Valerie is afraid that if she takes one step toward adulthood the whole safe structure of her life will come tumbling down. If each individual decision is considered and handled, that will not happen. The daughter has as much power as the mother in this merger. But Valerie diminishes hers by insisting that she would oppose her mother if the need arose—and it simply never has!

The process of separation from the Merger Mom requires introspection, trust in yourself, and a perpetual guard against self-deception.

## Strategies for Change

- It's time to question your relationship. All mothers enjoy their child's successes and want to offer comfort in their disappointments and all daughters want to share these parts of their lives. If, however, you go to Mom anxious about her reaction, if her opinion is more important than yours, if you do not know how *you* feel until *she* reacts, if you are afraid to celebrate your success without checking with her—it is time to question the validity of your relationship.
- If your choices are limited by Mom, take a good look at what is going on. The Merger Mom will often discourage her daughter's participation in activities that exclude the mother. The daughter feels afraid to do anything new or difficult lest she fail and disappoint her mom. She sticks to things she knows she can do and won't try anything new. She repeats what is familiar no matter how unsatisfying the pattern is.
- Watch for signs of too much emotional intertwining. If you are more concerned with her feelings than you are with your own, if you feel angry with her and sorry for her at the same time, if you feel the need to comfort *her* when *you* are hurt, if your triumphs and setbacks become hers, if your privacy is constantly invaded—these are signs that your emotional lives have become so intertwined that you have lost your ability to have your own feelings.

- Learn not to feel guilty about setting limits and establishing boundaries. Often, you will feel sadness at the possible loss of your mother's intrusion. You may doubt yourself and feel as if you are wrong to feel mistreated or resentful or angry. The very idea of taking action makes you anxious. These feelings are what keep you from looking at your situation with any clarity.
- Try to reconstruct your relationship with your mother as far back as you can recall. Was she withholding? Did she never give you quite enough attention or did you feel that the attention was phony? Search for specifics about the way she behaved and the way you responded. Try to spot ways of relating that you can connect to the present. Did she overprotect you? Did she constantly intrude? Did her worries make you fearful of the outside world? Try to remember whether she offered physical affection, encouragement, and true communication. If she did not, what did you do to get what you needed? You are probably still doing the same thing.
- Digging for the truth will not prevent you from loving your mother; it will enable you to love her honestly for perhaps the very first time. It will enable you to take some tiny steps toward what you really want and, with every move toward independence, with every decision you make on your own, you will learn that you are still safe and can find the courage to tackle the next one.

# 6

# The Seductress

## *The Developing Young Woman Turns to Dad*

ylvia Rosenfeld, a New York City psychotherapist who specializes in couples and sex therapy, says, "If you are left alone, you don't have to be encouraged to develop. It is nice to have the encouragement but, if you are not discouraged or pushed ahead, you look at your own body, explore, and find out what feels good. Kids learn about their bodies and how to get pleasure and they do it at their own pace.

"Parents are sexual people but that doesn't mean that you have to see them having sex. If they hold hands and are affectionate with one another, you get a sense that Mom and Dad are loving with each other. Mothers can talk to their daughters about sex without giving them details about their own sex lives. I had a patient whose mother would tell her that the father was forcing her to have sex. Kids don't need to know that.

"A lot of how you feel about your body has to do with how you were touched and held as a baby, how your mother changed your diaper, if she reacted in disgust when you touched yourself. What is equally important is how the human body is treated in the house, whether as something shameful or something normal—yet not flaunted.

"A lot depends on the child. In one of my patient's homes, they used to shower together as a family and, at a certain point, she could see that her son began to get uncomfortable with it. If a mother is attuned, she picks up what the kid is feeling. The problem with some mothers is that they are so undifferentiated, the child is like a part of them. So, if they need to walk about nude, they don't pick up that the kid might be feeling uncomfortable. Young girls go through periods where they are concerned about their breasts. If they are worried that theirs aren't big enough, if the mother flaunts her bigger breasts, the girls will have a problem. If you see that a child is uncomfortable, you stop doing it—not because it is something you want to stop doing. You stop doing it for the kid."

## Qualities of the Seductress

The Seductress is a mother whose skirts are too short, who uses too much makeup, who exposes too much cleavage. Everything she wears is designed to draw attention to herself. She carries off extravagant hats and lavish jewelry with style so that everyone always buzzes around her and she particularly sparkles whenever a man walks by.

> "I don't know if she was actually cheating on my father," says Sandy, forty-seven, "but boy, that's all she ever

talked about. Every man was good-looking. Every man, she claimed, was coming on to her. I used to die when she flirted with delivery boys and waiters. At parties, she would sit, scratching her hose with her long fingernails, sometimes lifting her skirt to do it, pretending to be oblivious, but every guy in the room would end up staring at her legs. At home, she strolled around naked. The rest of us wouldn't dare be seen in our underwear but she was Queen of the Jungle.

"She always hinted that my dad couldn't keep his hands off her and I remember, when I was a kid, we would be driving home late at night and he would try to grab a feel and she would squeal, 'Oh, Billy!' I was mortified and didn't understand what was going on. I didn't know if she really enjoyed it or not—and I still don't!

"The double messages were very confusing. One day, she was in the kitchen and my father came home from work. She was doing the dishes and he put his arms around her waist—just to greet her—and she reacted like he had whipped her around and kissed her passionately; she was giggling and blushing and whispering, 'Billy! Not in front of the children!' I was fifteen years old and I still remember how she sexualized everything and made sure we knew it—all the time giving off messages that it was taboo.

"With my sexuality, she was no help at all. I got my first period during the night and woke up and thought I had died. I looked down and called for my mom. She came into my room and I flipped up the blanket and she said, 'Go into the bathroom!' Then, I heard her yelling to my sister who was four years older, 'Take care of Sandy!' That was it. My sister threw me a box, threw me a belt,

and screamed at me, 'I want this back!' I never really
went to my mom for anything like that from then on.
But she never stopped giving off the clues.

"She's seventy now and, just the other day, we're talking on the phone. She, of course, was complaining about
my dad. 'Maybe I shouldn't tell you this,' she says—it's
supposed to be a complaint but it comes out more like
a boast—'But, sexually, he's worse than ever!'

# What's Behind Mom's Behavior?

Behind the Seductress is an insecure woman. She wants to
have every man—or at least his attention—because it is a
way to feel powerful. She wants to be seen as the best and
the sexiest because she does not feel that way, no matter
how many conquests she makes. Some women go so far as
having a round of affairs, some actually have a passionate
relationship with their husbands (which they boast about
shamelessly), but, either way, it is not enough. The Seductress complains of feeling deprived and lonely and restless.
No man makes her feel loved. No triumph relieves the
emptiness she feels inside.

Her emotions can explode into terrifying rages and inexplicable mood changes. She romances her husband and acts
like a princess, but she can turn vicious and demeaning in a
second. Because she is so self-involved and insecure, she
reacts to others only in terms of how much they reaffirm her
position as top dog. The daughter's responses also touch
sensitive nerve endings, so that these mother–daughter conflicts have a frightening explosiveness. Both mother and
daughter live in fear of one another—and for good reason.

"Sexualized energy controls the household," says Sylvia
Rosenfeld. "Perhaps something is not going on between the

mother and father so she puts all this energy in the wrong places, particularly on the child. These mothers convey a message of sexuality being this wild, uncontrollable thing because they can't contain their own. The girls get the message that sexuality is something that has to be bridled; that sex is bad because it destroys things.

"The fact is a girl's sexual fantasies can be enjoyable but she doesn't have to act on them. You can feel great passion, great desire without acting on it. But if your mother felt anger and couldn't contain it, felt sexuality and always expressed it, either you repress your sexuality or, when it starts to come out, you are not able to feel it without letting it get out of control."

## The Healthy Dad and the Developing Young Woman

Let's talk about dads for a change. Even with a neurotic mother, daughters who have felt loved and admired by their fathers tend to be less scarred. Whatever mother is up to, Dad can offer a bridge to the outside world. How he responds to his daughter—especially in adolescence—can either help her to move on toward caring men and her own identity or can imprison her in lifelong dependency on others.

The good father loves his daughter, supports her, is pleased by her accomplishments, and encourages her to venture forth. With his backing, it is easier for her to have the courage of her convictions, to be curious, and to explore new aspects of her inner and outer worlds.

To the growing girl, Dad can be a model for achievement, independence, and ambition if, no matter how much his daughter molds her identity on him, her accomplishments are not threatening to him. If Dad can see his daughter as who she is, rather than as an extension of himself, it enhances her ability to form her own identity.

The healthy father is not the kind of man who really wanted a son, who overvalues men, and who devalues the feminine attributes of his daughter. The good dad admires his daughter's looks and her interest in how she looks without becoming seductive. In her teens, when a girl is experimenting with sexuality, he does not allow himself to be seduced but neither does he withdraw from his daughter. He is able to admire her attempts at womanhood, while making it clear that he finds her mother attractive and that the mother is the one who is his mate.

As a five year old, the daughter can flirt with her dad, sit on his lap, claim that she loves him more than Mom—and the healthy mother's security is not threatened. As the daughter grows, she and her father can have their own shared interests; he coaches her sports team and they do other things that don't include Mom. A comfortable mother can allow them to have such a relationship and the daughter is relieved because the mother does not resent it.

When there is conflict between mother and daughter, this father tries to understand his daughter. He talks to her about what is going on, rather than blaming her. He makes it clear that he need not take sides in order to support and love her. As an adolescent, the girl begins to recognize that Mom and Dad have a good thing going. In the sexual area, she cannot win. Every daughter of a healthy, happy marriage has to come to terms with that. If she gets caught in a sexual triangle, or if she opts out of it by denying her own sexuality, she stays bonded with her mother in a guilt-ridden way.

## The Seductress and the Developing Young Woman

The Seductress frequently sees other women, including her own child, as threats and competitors. She views her daughter not for who she is but only as a potential audience. To the Seductress, the daughter's purpose is to admire the mother's conquests, despite the fact that the Seductress usually makes a display of being "one of the kids."

> "My mother wanted to do everything I did with my friends," says Tanya, age twenty-eight. "She said she wanted to have fun but I sensed the competition. I saw the lies. She had these long fingernails which she painted blood red, and I have vivid memories of being afraid of them. To this day, I keep my nails short and refuse to wear any polish. "

The Seductress has difficulty encouraging her child to be feminine. Instead, her own abilities at seduction and flirtation overwhelm her daughter's efforts. The girl ends up feeling ungainly and awkward and tends to retreat.

> "She wouldn't let me wear lipstick or Mary Janes," continues Tanya, "while she wore low-cut blouses and never went anywhere without high heels. I dressed in baggy clothes because I didn't want to be seen. I was not comfortable when attention was on me and I always had the radar out so as not to upset her."

When the daughter of the Seductress reaches puberty, her development is seen as a threat to the mother's power in the household. The daughter's need to maintain the relationship curtails her ability to value her own attractiveness. She may gain a great deal of weight, then go on a binge diet.

> "I remember going out with my mom when she was all dressed up. Men on the street would whistle. I was

jealous and felt ugly. This was followed by a hunger to be better than she was—at anything! I would show her what a mistake she had made about me. Then I would feel guilty and begin to wonder if there really was something wrong with me."

## Caught Between Mom and Dad

The daughter who is embarrassed by her mother's exhibitionism often wears clothes that cover up her body; she camouflages herself. She may choose to wear jeans and flannel shirts. She retreats from boys because she has difficulty handling her own sexuality, confusing it with being a "vamp" like Mom.

She often sees herself as having more in common with her father than her mother. Dad and daughter have an alliance, often in mutual protection against the mother. Perhaps they talk books; she admires his intellectual traits and models herself after him. On some level, however, she senses her mother's contempt for her father, which exacerbates the hidden tensions.

"My mother said that all men are dirt and even told me negative stories about my father," says Tanya. "I wanted her to tell me about one point when they had been happy. She denied ever being happy. She said he tried to get her not to have children. Imagine telling that to me! She would lie to my father so that he wouldn't know how much things cost and I hated that. She was nothing but a front, a woman who was essentially empty, that's why she lied. My heart went out to my dad."

The husband of the Seductress can really like his daughter and she can really like him but, if he does not stand up to Mom, his daughter ends up feeling that she has to protect him against the mother's wrath and the situation worsens. If the mother flaunts sex with Dad, the daughter recognizes the inappropriateness of this, yet she feels stimulated, curious, and guilty. All sexuality can become uncomfortable and confusing for the daughter of the Seductress.

"I always knew when my parents were having sex," says Tanya. "They'd get up on Saturday mornings and close the door. At the time, I didn't understand the sounds. I thought my mother didn't like it. All sorts of things about sex turned me off. Afterward, she would come out and cook breakfast. Without even washing her hands! Why didn't she wash her hands? I couldn't stand it!"

Even the Seductress who demeans her husband does not want her daughter to have him. But if a young girl does not understand, on some level, that her parents have a reasonably satisfying sex life, she has missed out on an important lesson. She becomes afraid of showing up her mother by developing an erotic life of her own and she has to deal with frightening fantasies.

"In my secret life," Tanya concludes, "I wanted to be a queen. I wanted to be arrogant and snub my nose at every woman on the street. I wanted to be superior, to devastate men and brag about my conquests so that other women would envy me, so that my mother would throw herself on the sofa and sob. I wanted her to kill herself and I would know that I drove her to it; that she ended up so lonely and desperate there was no other way out. That's how strong my anger was. What was I supposed to do about that?"

Rather than competing with Mom for Dad's affection, learning that she cannot win, and moving on to other men from there, the daughter of the Seductress removes herself from the competition altogether. The possibility that she might triumph is too dangerous, her mother would be too jealous, and the consequences would be devastating. She neuters herself in order to maintain her relationship with Dad and not compete with Mom.

"When someone cuts off her sexuality," says Rosenfeld, "it is not always a sexual thing. It can be a way of setting limits, having some control. There is no control in a household where you do not know what is going to set your mother off because anything can. Sometimes, the uncontrollable anger and the sexuality get fused together in the child's mind. These mothers aren't angry, they are rageful— so the daughters do not get angry because anger seems dangerous. It's good to have a household where people fight, where they show anger and then resolution of anger. Anger is not a problem but what these daughters see is parents dumping a lot of rage and that is scary."

## What's in Store for the Daughter of the Seductress?

This girl turns often into a "good kid"—she toes the line in order to avoid her mother's frightening rage. She becomes highly proficient in every area except femininity and sensuality, where the danger of competing with Mom is all too clear.

> "I turned myself into an outstanding student—self-sacrificing, honest, self-sufficient—all those words that don't mean a damn to other kids, especially to boys," says Iris, now thirty-six. "I got involved in frantic never-ending activity in high school, took over for my mom

with my brothers and sisters, developed a rigid sense of
pride, a perfectionism. I learned to take charge. It was
easier to be in control than to just want."

As a grown woman, the daughter of the Seductress
tends to get involved with married men because they are
unavailable. When the man leaves his wife for her, she loses
interest. She never really wanted her father to leave her
mother; the guilt would have been unbearable. So she plays
out this drama from the past with her married lover until
the situation comes too close to her fears.

Perhaps she falls in love with homosexuals and thinks
that she can change them. By loving only unavailable
men, she will not show her mom up, she will not compete
with her, because she will not have a man of her own.
When only Mom can shine, the tenuous peace will be
maintained.

It may be that the daughter's bond with Dad is so
intense that she picks only inferior men as lovers so as not
to threaten their secret relationship. Thus, she can continue
to cherish the fantasy that she would have made a better
wife to her father than Mom did.

Sometimes, the daughter of the Seductress can find sexual satisfaction only with men with whom there is always
the threat of rejection and explosion. In this way, she titil-
lates herself with the possibility of Mom's furious reaction,
plays out the battle, and feels relieved because she has sur-
vived. She gets turned on only by stolen sex, where there is
danger, and where there is the constant question of who is
going to dump whom first. As soon as a relationship develops, she becomes anxious. Closeness to this woman means
claustrophobia.

Many of these women grow up depressed and wary of
romance altogether. They marry but do not value sex. They
are nonorgasmic and passive; they "tolerate" their husband's

sexual demands because they are such good girls in every area of life, or they may be so focused on pleasing their partners that they lose touch with what feels good to them.

The daughter of the Seductress has the secret expectation that her desires, although unexpressed to herself and to others, will mysteriously be fulfilled. She is therefore free to remain blind to her feelings, to avoid testing them or expressing them, and she expects to be loved and admired because she is so devoted to others.

This woman sees all authority figures as hostile and harsh. She might perform well at work or at school, but she never develops the capacity for independent, creative thinking. She defers to the opinions of others in order to maintain her relationships. She wants to be sweet and shy, clean and neat. In this way, she denies her anger with her mother, which the rebel is so actively playing out. But she complains that she feels like a feather in the wind, buffeted by forces beyond her control, dependent on her husband or her lover. Without the approval of another, she feels small and inadequate. She has no trust in her own opinion of herself. By cutting herself off from her sexuality, she has numbed a huge chunk of her inner experience. As a result, she feels lonely and helpless. Sometimes, she is subject to temper tantrums or crying jags for which she feels guilty. She longs to return to infancy and the fantasy of the all-loving mother.

The rages of childhood can turn the daughter of the Seductress into a control freak, a compulsive housekeeper. Her anger is expressed in picky, petty ways, which leave others mystified. When this woman cannot control the situation, she blows up; her behavior as inexplicable to herself as it is to others. Unfortunately, these indirect explosions do nothing to release the feelings, the sexual confusion, the fear of lack of control. Arguments can never be resolved because the real cause of the conflict—Mom—is no longer on the scene. Having no other way to express her rage, this daughter turns it on herself and becomes highly self-critical.

Or she may get involved with men who express it for her: men who are jealous the way her mother was, who explode the way she did, who threaten to abandon her the way her mother seemed to. Her fantasy is that, if she can control these men, her fears from the past will vanish.

None of these resolutions is satisfactory. All serve to preserve the status quo of childhood, to keep Dad idealized and unthreatened, to pacify Mom's rage, to muffle her own rage—and at what a cost. With the loss of her sensuality, she has also sacrificed all possibilities for real joy, spontaneity, and pleasure in her life.

Kay is a sixty-three-year-old woman in trim black trousers, a tailored white shirt. She wears no makeup, her hair is no-nonsense short, yet her voice is wispy with a trace of her southern roots.

"My mother was beautiful, a perfect housekeeper and a perfect entertainer, extremely concentrated on my father, though he was totally dominated by her. She would say things like, 'Dwight! You can't think that!' She was a southern lady so at ten o'clock in the morning she'd be dressed the way I would go to a cocktail party. Then she dressed again for dinner by the time he came home from work.

"I was very afraid of her; always trying to be what she wanted me to be, at the same time constantly observing to see when this dark cloud of fury would come over her—not understanding anything about what it was. I found out many years later that she was alcoholic but I had no idea at that time. That was the way life was.

"She would have these attacks of fury, hardly ever directed at me but often at my governess, whom I adored and who probably saved my life. It was she who gave me unconditional love and my mother hated her. I was caught between them and was always trying to protect the servants or my father or my brother. Her rage would be aimed at any of these people and I was always observing, waiting because I thought it would be better if I saw it coming. I still do that. I'm terribly aware of tensions in people. I'm a psychologist. I thought that if I watched it would be easier.

"My father was an alcoholic, too, but he was a sweet one. She got mean. The entire family was afraid of her, the way she needed to be treated like a queen. She needed to have people around her constantly, making her feel good. You had to think how wonderful everything she said was and, if you didn't, she'd be angry.

"Generally speaking, she seduced my friends. They adored her and didn't see the bad side at all. I have a close friend from childhood who says that my mother saved her life from her own difficult mother and tyrannical father, and that my mother was always standing up for her. Many years later, she came into my life again and ran into this mean mother of mine and was just heartbroken because she remembered her as being so affirming to her.

"I don't think I ever admitted to myself that I didn't adore my mother, even though I knew I was unhappy and liked to get away. I thought that it was my fault. She was so charming and it was like there was some sort of a halo around her. She said that every man in Savannah was in love with her—maybe it was true.

So many people adored her, which made it harder for me than if she had been unbearable.

"But there were these scenes, which usually happened at dinner. She would get furious about something and march upstairs to her room and we would all be left in solitude and suspense. Sometimes my father would get mad and drive away. When he was older, my brother would do the same and that would make her upset and frightened. She was always allowed to leave, but no one was allowed to leave her.

"My refuge was to go into the woods and be with my horses. I would sob on my little pony's neck and tell her what was going on; that I wanted to be what would make her happy, which meant to be the perfect child, so I tried to be good, to do everything well, to always smile.

"I wanted to be a boy. I didn't want to be like any of the women I knew; lots of them were like my mother. But there must have been a time earlier when I wanted her—I always wanted her. But I never had dolls. Clothes were terribly important to her and she dressed me properly but not prettily. I felt best in blue jeans, with my horses, outside, and in nature. That's where I felt most attractive. That's still true.

"My parents were married for fifty-eight years and, as far as any of us can find out, he never strayed, nor did she. There were men around; one was a painter who was probably between my age and hers and he adored her. In that era, as long as she had a stream of admirers around, it didn't have to go further. Still, it was demeaning to my father.

"The first time my father ever told me that I looked nice was when I was about twenty-five. I was coming down the stairs and my mother had gone ahead to a party. He said, 'You look pretty,' and I thought, 'I've never heard him say that before and how strange that she's not here.' I think she was jealous of any attention he paid to anyone. I talked to my father a lot but always about impersonal subjects—politics and economics— all of my energies were channeled into being an intellectual person. But he never stood up for me and I really resented it.

"I was always a rebel in an underhanded kind of way, going off and doing everything she didn't want me to, not being very dressy, finding the wrong boyfriends. I went as far away as I could—to boarding school at fourteen and I never lived at home again. From there I went to Wellesley and, in my junior year, I went to Spain, where I married at twenty-four. I had always identified with the marginal elements, people who are not quite accepted, and my husband was one of these.

"Amazingly enough, Mother accepted my strange husband. I thought that they would kill each other but they got along very well. He was an alcoholic like her and they were both people whose word had to be followed by everybody around them. Both extroverts, very critical, both tyrants.

"He was a brilliant Spaniard and basically what attracted me was that he was all involved in this search for the meaning of life. I felt like I had married the opposite of my father because Dad was clean, orderly, and easygoing and my husband was kind of dirty and disorderly and had no friends. But basically I had married a tyrant like my mother.

"I was totally tied to him, even though it was an awful marriage, a sick love–hate relationship. Eventually I found out that he was having an affair with his secretary and, thank god, he left me. But it took my pride rather than years of total noncommunication to get me out of it.

"I wildly blamed him. I blamed him pretty much from the beginning. I couldn't believe that this man was so difficult and irresponsible and unresponsive and I kept thinking that he could change. It really made me angry, this business about his secretary, but it freed me. I had never expressed anger with my mother but here I was, hysterical and screaming and crying and it was all blaming, blaming, blaming—but never with my mother.

"The only time I remember standing up to her was over an inconsequential thing. I was probably thirty, living in Madrid. My parents were visiting and she made some comment about wearing dark shoes with a light dress and I said, 'I wish you wouldn't criticize me all the time,' and she went into a fury, stood up, and said, 'Dwight, we are leaving right now. I have never heard anything so terrible in my life.' They left my house, went to the airport, and flew home. Talk about abandonment. That was what I knew as a little girl would happen if I stood up to her.

"Soon I had a new man in my life. This man thought that I was beautiful, wonderful. He did all the things that my husband hadn't done. But that didn't last very long. Then I got into another relationship that lasted twenty years: another difficult man, another alcoholic, another love–hate connection, first his getting rid of me and then my getting tired of him. I have never been able to sustain a relationship with a man who is nice, who loves me and is kind. I am totally turned off by it.

I have always had the kind of relationships that were very passionate, along with a lot of hate and, in the end, just awful.

"With a nicer man, I have this strange feeling of unreality and of being a little bit bored. This happens over and over again. I try to change the pattern and relate in a different way to another man, but I feel as though I'm dead. Does that mean I can never have passion in a different kind of relationship? Probably not as much as I've had in these stormy affairs, but I'm beginning to think there are lots of nicer things. I have to accept that no one is going to come along and give me the unconditional love that I didn't have. Except myself.

"I'm going through this now with my eldest son who has been living at home for the last month. He is an alcoholic and he's just left his wife and three children to come home in pain to live with me. This has thrown me tremendously. It's been difficult and I've been going back, back, back—first to my husband who left me with my three boys, but probably to my mother and my fears of her abandoning me.

"I'm going to have to tell my son he has to leave. It's not good for me, probably not good for him. I realized that what I feel around him is—invisible. I'm not there for him as far as my feelings are concerned or my views. I'm just a provider. I've always felt invisible: as a little girl, as a wife, and now as a mother. I said to him, 'I don't ever again want to live with someone who I care about and feel invisible.' I don't think that he understood but it was nice to be able to say it."

# Separation: Accepting the Loss

As you extricate yourself from the threads of the past, there is going to be a loss. The myths of childhood have an overwhelming power and giving them up costs. The world as you saw it through your young eyes had a drama and a sparkle; joys were high, lows were terrifying. Adults had unimaginable powers. The world had the feel of a fairy tale. The pleasures of reality are often subtler. Women who have been entangled in the past often find that when they finally give up the scenario and refuse to act it out with lovers and husbands and children, this childhood glow diminishes.

As the adult daughter of the Seductress, the excitement of the drama has often added to the sexuality and the romance of your life. The threat of danger in your relationships provides the kick. Without it, life seems boring. You hang onto your childhood vision because you think it is more attractive and appealing than everyday life.

As you try to separate yourself from the myths of your mother, from the intensity of your childhood feelings, you are going to feel a loss. To walk out on the drama may leave you feeling empty for a time, without an identity because that is all you know. You'll feel anxious and bored and restless while you learn about the pleasures of real life. It takes awhile, like going off salt, before you can learn to appreciate the real taste of things. The pleasures of adulthood—setting up your own goals and achieving them, choosing friends who support you rather than use you, finding a man who has no need to dominate, facing your feelings rather than running away—are not as glamorous as being the heroine in the silent screen melodrama of your childhood.

In order to separate from Mom the Seductress, you also must separate from her surrogates, from the scenario, from your needs for revenge, from the fantasy that you can conquer and destroy, from the wish to go back and replay scenes so that they will turn out differently. Awareness of that can be scary and disappointing; it takes some real growth to accept this situation and move on.

# Strategies for Change

- Take a good look at your past behaviors. The daughter of the Seductress often tries to "escape" either by idealizing her mother, passively accepting her own fate as a nonsexual being, or by rebelling and seething with hatred of her mother.
- Stop clinging to your rage. Your rage at your mother may have become your connection to her and you cling to it, you feel "dead" without it. However, your identity is so tied to her image that if you cannot accept your mother's faults with some understanding and compassion—if you cannot find peace with the past—you'll never be at peace with yourself.

  You may be harshly self-critical and unforgiving of your own faults; unable to take pleasure and pride in your femininity. If you are so wrapped up in rage at your mother, how can you make use of the admirable traits she did have? You must face your rage and then you must find some way of handling it, other than in constantly playing it out with her or with men.
- Trying to control your mother will not produce a successful resolution. "As an adult," says Sylvia Rosenfeld, "you might be so involved with trying to control your mother you avoid taking control of your own life. You may be powerless in terms of changing her but you are not powerless in terms of taking care of yourself, protecting your-

self, learning about your own sexuality, and putting the focus on you instead of on other people."

- Learn to develop new skills with your mate. "We usually choose mates," Rosenfeld concludes, "who are a combination of the positive and negative characteristics of those who took care of us and who fill in the gaps for the parts of ourselves that haven't developed. So, if you are a retiring kind of person whose socialization skills have never developed you are going to marry the very social person. These partnerships can actually succeed if both people want to work on their issues. Because when the tyrant learns to control his temper, it's good for him and it is healing for the person coming from the parent who couldn't. Power struggles develop when you want to kill off that quality like it was killed off in you. But when people decide they want to make their marriage succeed and are committed to growing and meeting each other's needs, it can work very well."

# 7

# The Critic

## The Young Woman Gains Self-Esteem

*L*ittle girls are different from little boys. Because of the intensity of the mother–daughter connection, because of the physical and sexual identity involved in the relationship, girls place more importance on bonding. A little boy's most crucial identification is with his father, but a daughter has the same kind of body and sexual identity as her mother. She and her mother share the roles that society imposes on women. Between mothers and sons there is not the sense of sameness that entangles mothers and daughters. As one mother said, "A daughter will get mad at you and, when she's finished, she'll say, 'And I hate your hair that way!' Sons don't need to disavow you as well as criticize you."

Autonomy becomes a prime goal in the early lives of boys while girls develop greater interest in relationships. A woman can succeed in any job that a man can—but she might go about it differently. She may win through negotiation and diplomacy, not through the need to overpower. A woman can be a caregiver and still be independent—as long as she does not hide behind the role to the detriment of her own needs—which is what the daughter of the Critic often does.

## Qualities of the Critic

The Critic views her daughter as a reflection of herself so that every imperfection mortifies her. She wants the girl to be perfect, not for her own sake, but because only then can the young woman be the image of the princess the mother sees as herself. Since this mother's self-esteem is so low, she finds little to praise in the daughter. There is rarely any positive feedback so the critical attacks are intense.

The danger is deceptive because the attack is usually not dramatic, but constant and insidious. With her perpetual assaults, the Critic eats away at your confidence, at your ability to make decisions. You begin to wonder if she really said what she said, if she really meant what it sounded like, if you are overreacting, if she is right and you are wrong.

In a 1996 interview, superstar Barbra Streisand, still smarting from ancient wounds, said:

> When I was eighteen, I sang at Bon Soir, and when
> my mother came to see me her comment was: "Your
> voice is very thin. You need eggs in your milk to make
> your voice strong . . ."[1]

---

1. Bernard Weinraub, "Barbra Streisand, Still Not Pretty Enough," *New York Times,* November 13, 1996, p. C15.

When Streisand asked her mother if she'd been pretty as a baby, her mother responded, "All babies are pretty." Streisand reacted to these constant critical attacks by turning into a high achiever who requires control over everything in her life and art so that she will never again be subject to attack and humiliation.

## What's Behind Mom's Behavior?

The Critic's low self-esteem causes her to seek perfection in her daughter to cover up her own empty feelings. She hopes the daughter's attainments will make her feel more whole herself. Ironically, her efforts to prod her daughter to higher achievement come across—to the daughter—as demoralizing judgments.

"My mother was the cerebral one, with a law degree and two doctorates," says Amelia, a woman in her fifties, "and somehow she made me feel that I could never be that good. If I got a B plus, she'd say 'Why didn't you get an A?'

"But such feelings were never discussed in our house—not my feelings and certainly not hers. Before she died, she had to have an operation and, the night before, in her hospital room, she was reading the papers. She read newspapers from all over the world. A young priest came in and said, 'Mrs. Graham, is there anything you'd like to talk to me about?' She looked at him with utter contempt and said, 'Unless you want to discuss the situation in the Middle East, no.' She was that closed off!

"After my mom died, I found letters to her from relatives saying isn't it wonderful that Amelia did this and that. She wrote to her mother that I had the lead in a school play but she never said to me, 'That's great.' My daughter, who was very close to her, thinks she was depressed her whole life and that actually makes some sense to me. Maybe she was so judgmental because she was depressed and it had nothing at all to do with me!"

It is the combination of a mother's poor self-image, her need to see herself and her child as perfect, and a total denial of her feelings that can turn a mother into a Critic.

## The Healthy Mother and the Young Woman

One of the crucial tasks of adolescence is giving up parents as the be-all and end-all of one's existence. The adolescent girl has to learn to see her parents for who they actually are and not as the ideals she made them out to be as a young child. Hand in hand with this new awareness, the adolescent reevaluates her own capacities and limitations.

A challenging moment comes when the young girl has to face the fact that she is not going to win Dad away from Mom. If she wants romantic love in her life, she has to get out of the house and find a man of her own. With this news come insights that the good mother has been helping her prepare to accept her entire life: Mom's love is not unconditional; there are limits. Mom has her own needs. Dad and Mom have a relationship, part of which excludes the daughter. Some desires—many of which the adolescent is just beginning to acknowledge—will have to be fulfilled elsewhere.

Her job in life, it eventually becomes clear, is not to compete with Mom, not to replace her, not even to replicate her. In a crucial area, she cannot step into her mother's shoes. Romantic and sexual exploration is not a journey she can take with Mom at her side. She is now her own person, running her own life, defining her own desires, and getting them satisfied on her own terms.

She has come face to face with the reality of adulthood. The world does not revolve around her; she is one of many and her powers are limited. What is important to her may not be important to everyone else. Whatever she wants she will have to work for and just because she wants it does not mean that she will get it. If she doesn't get it, she'll have to find a way to go on. If she does, it will not be the answer to her every prayer.

With this awareness the myth of the idealized all-powerful, all-protective, all-loving mother comes tumbling to the ground. There is a loss of fantasy, a sense of aloneness that is part and parcel of being an adult. However, nature has a way of kicking us into new stages of life—whether we want to get there or not. Just as the infant follows the impulse to crawl without knowing the goal, the young woman reaches for adulthood. She is only dimly aware of what she is losing and of what is to be gained. The conflict within her produces strain but she struggles on.

In addition, the daughter of a healthy mother has had many years to prepare for this moment. She has developed other resources, found other supports. She has made friends with whom she can share her experiments in independence. She has found role models, connected with groups, and learned that she can manage without Mom. She is not alone nor is she as helpless as an infant.

She has developed a sense of mastery: the knowledge that she can do things, that she can measure her own abilities and know what to aim for. She has a good idea of what success she can expect and what will require further work. She can trust her impulses about when she is safe and when she is not and does not always need her parent's protection. She has developed her own sense of right and wrong and can rely on that. She has absorbed many images of womanhood; some would meet her mother's approval, some would not.

Although she now knows that the loving arms of her mother will not always be there, she also knows that love can be found from others: from friends, from a man. But the young woman has to find it in herself before she can expect it from anyone else. She has to take pleasure in her accomplishments, work for her own satisfaction. No praise from others can mean as much as her own inner strength and self-esteem.

The healthy young woman emerges from puberty knowing who she is and appreciating her uniqueness. While she has lost the fantasy that she will have omnipotent, omniscient love in her life, she has also lost the need for it. She is able to replace the constant and abiding love of her mother with her love of herself. She has developed strong self-esteem.

# The Critic and the Young Woman

While the task of adolescence is to discover your capabilities, your potential, and your sense of pleasurable femininity, the Critic reinforces your identity as helpless, dependent, and forever a child.

"When I was in eighth grade," says Belinda, forty-four, "I was in the school talent show. I got up to play the piano, did all right for three-quarters of the way through, then hit a wrong note. I recovered and went on. I didn't think it was bad. I got nice applause at the end so I was pleased. I went to sit beside my parents and my mother said under her breath, 'You made a mistake! I heard you!' And the whole thing was ruined. I felt like I was a complete failure. Everybody had heard the mistake.

> Nobody had heard the good playing. That was emblematic of the way she was."

When you grow up, the Critic finds fault with the men in your life, up to and including your husband. She is not a Competitor. She doesn't want your job or your man because, in her eyes, they are not good enough. In fact, nothing is. The Critic thinks she is praising you with her high standards. In fact, she is putting you down. Sometimes she does both in such a confusing way that you cannot figure out what's right and what's wrong.

> Belinda says that when she was dating her future husband, her mother hated him for two reasons: "One, she didn't want me to marry him and, two, he wasn't proposing fast enough!"

When you believe the critical mother, when you allow her voice to nest in your brain, you learn to see yourself the way she does—but you can't be angry with her, you can't hate her because, after all, how could you possibly survive alone? So you turn the anger against yourself. If you stray from any of Mom's rigid codes of conduct—and there are millions of them—eventually the criticism does not come out in Mom's voice, it comes out as your own guilt.

> Belinda vividly remembers the year she got all As in high school. What did her mother say? "Brains aren't everything. Good thing they're not grading character."
> "You'd think I would have hauled off and socked her. But no, at sixteen, I couldn't claim that I had an unimpeachable character; she had zeroed in on yet another of my weaknesses. She always had the knack of doing that. At college, every letter I sent to her was returned

with the punctuation and misspellings corrected. When I had moved away from home, I would come back to visit and I would swear, on the plane, that this time everything would go smoothly. We would embrace for one moment of warmth and love. Then she would pull away and say, 'Is this how you dress all the time?'

"I always wore my skirts too long, she said. I looked like a European grandmother because I wore black tights. 'I just don't want you to embarrass me,' she'd moan. I'd bound down the stairs to meet a guy and she'd be sitting there. 'I hope you're not going to wear that skirt,' were her farewell words.

"And my weight, of course. We'll be sitting around after Thanksgiving dinner. I'll reach for a cookie and she'll say, 'Oh sure, eat some more cookies!'—this in front of the entire family. Or she'll say, 'I don't understand how you'll wear a bathing suit this vacation. We'll probably have to go to a special store where they can make one for you.' Then she'll laugh. I go home to cry—and eat. If I wear something big to hide the weight, she'll say, 'What are you, Omar the Tent Maker?'

"The biggest joke used to be about me and my sister, Megan. The way my mother told it, giggling with delight, 'When Megan was born she was this beautiful baby and I was so happy, but Belinda was this homely little thing and it took me the longest time to get used to her!' The first time she met my future husband, she told him how, when I was in high school, I couldn't spell and she used to have to type my papers for me.

"I explain this to people, they say, 'What are you complaining about? She's a lovely woman who wanted the best for you. These are minor faults.' My own aunt, my mother's sister, never understood—although my mother treated her badly, too. But she was able to handle it because she was less afraid of her—she wasn't her mother. I could never make anyone believe how my mother was mean in tiny, petty, never-ending ways. It was impossible for me to get her approval."

## What's in Store for the Critic's Daughter?

The grown daughter of the Critic does not always become a super achiever like Streisand. Often she tends to "cocoon"; staying home, watching television, reading, avoiding people. She's afraid of the world, ashamed, guilty, and unable to acknowledge her needs. She becomes excessively dependent on affirmation from men, from groups, and finds it hard to value achievement that does not please others.

The "cocooning" daughter is so afraid to be on her own that she avoids competition and achievement. She fears that success will cause her to lose connectedness, sees ambition as unfeminine, and avoids any desire for power or control because these are attributes that she connects to her dominating mother.

The daughter of the Critic lends her credit cards to the wrong guys, is always chauffeuring people to airports, stays up nights writing term papers for boyfriends, and spends hours on the phone negotiating spats between friends. She believes that people will love her only if she serves their needs. Unfortunately for her, they may become dependent on her services, but that is not love.

The cycle gets worse. When the daughter of the Critic withdraws from competitive achievement because she fears failure—or maybe success—she ensures that her self-esteem will drop and that she'll continue to be dependent on others. Her major goal often becomes a relationship with a man to fill the gap she feels inside. She settles for a sub-servient position as a wife. Her husband makes all the deci-sions. He controls the money. Their social life revolves around his friends. He is probably super-critical and she lives in fear of his disapproval.

The Critic has an easy time maintaining control over you for all of your life. Faced with her latest comments about your clothes, your hair, your job, you tend to regress and feel the insecurity you felt as a child, which gives her all the more power. No matter how hard you try, it's never good enough and you always end up doubting yourself.

"I went home for a wedding," Belinda continues, "and, since my mother complains that I don't know how to dress, that I always look like a slob, that I'm never put together enough—and on and on and on—I planned it all to a tee. The dress was appropriate. I had the matching stockings. I went out and bought a new bra. I had all the right accessories and I hung it all up in the closet ready for me to wear. I put my pearls—pearls that were from my parents, of course—on the hanger, too.

"I returned from visiting relatives and my mother was banging around in the kitchen so I knew something was wrong. My father sidles up to me and gives me this velvet pouch, mumbling, 'I have an extra one of these. Why don't you use it?' All of a sudden, my mother starts screaming, 'Who hangs pearls on a hanger? Who hangs four-thousand dollar pearls on a wire hanger? Do you know that's how they break? You are never going to get another set of pearls like that. Your husband is not going to be able to buy you pearls like this. Who does this? I don't understand!'

"I had thought I was such a clever person; not only had I hung up all my clothes, I had hung up my pearls. I was being so efficient, had thought every last thing through. And yet I had done this thing, and I had the feeling that every time I made such a stupid mistake, I must have been doing it on purpose. I didn't get angry because this woman is out of her mind, but I wondered how I was playing into this. I felt kind of shaky. I don't know if the answer is to take her on when she gets like this. There is no getting back at her. There is no making up with her. It's over but I am still going through . . ."

This woman, trying so hard to see things clearly, bursts into child-like tears. But why did Belinda need to feel like a failure because of her mistake? She did bring a suitable outfit so she wasn't incompetent. Should someone who got criticized for one mistake feel totally inept? Should she subject herself to more pain by rejecting herself? If Belinda could have maintained her assessment of the situation and not have joined her mother's overreaction, she would not have the need to burst into tears every time she remembers.

On the other hand, many talented and creative people try to protect themselves but still feel insecure and vulnerable. They are constantly saying to the world "Look at me! See how good I am!" because their mothers were so negative. They need to control every aspect of their work, become perfectionists, take forever to make decisions because their internal critic cannot allow their initial impulse to be trusted. They learn to rely only on their own efforts, to depend on no one—in work as well as their private life. They give up all hope of being understood and instead focus their efforts on gaining attention and a sense of self-worth through their achievements.

## Self-Esteem

Self-esteem involves a person's estimate of how good she is at what she does, how she looks, what she produces, who she is. It is her own measure of her chances of success in personal relationships, in how others will respond to her, in how she will meet the expectations of herself and of others, and in how she will cope if she does not meet them. Self-esteem is deeply involved with having a realistic picture of who she is and what she can do, being reasonably pleased with that picture, and feeling confident that she can improve where work is needed.

A woman with strong self-esteem can handle rejection, competition, and humiliation. Therefore, she tries for more and achieves more than someone with low self-esteem. People respond to her better. Her inner world creates her outer world.

In order to develop healthy self-esteem, not only do you require loving, supportive parents, but you also need to see your parents in light of their true abilities and limitations. Many young adults get stuck here—unable to de-idealize their parents and move on. If your picture of Mom remains either romanticized as all-loving or resented as always judgmental, you cannot come to a sense of your own power, you are not free to develop a realistic picture of yourself. You must demystify your mother so that you are not measuring yourself against a mirage. If you live perpetually under the cloud of some impossible ideal—or are fearful of her constant judgment—self-criticism, self-punishment, and painful feelings of inferiority are the likely result. In addition, your every thrust toward establishing a separate identity will lead to guilt, anxiety, and depression because you fear the loss of your mother's love.

# Separation: Changing Your Self-Image

The worst thing that you can do is to try to increase your low self-esteem by gaining your mother's approval. The Critic cannot give it and the more you beg, plead, and insist, the more she will bulldoze your efforts. In order for you to repair yourself, you must first allay your self-doubt. Ironically, the more hostile the relationship you have with your mother, the more self-critical you will become. These feelings keep you tied to Mom.

To learn how to handle conflict with your mother, first try to handle your own inner conflict. Question the image you have of yourself being inadequate, powerless, and acceptable only if you tend to others. Only you can give yourself self-esteem; it is in the very definition of what it is.

Often you are more understanding and supportive to others than you are to yourself. Once you have absorbed your mother's opinions and criticisms, you tend to use them to chastise yourself. If you hear yourself using childish words (like "dumb" or "stupid") about your efforts or expressions of your mother's (like "you're stubborn as a mule!"), you are drawing on assumptions learned in child-hood. As soon as you hear her voice in your head, recognize where it is coming from and lay off the self-punishment. Your mother's rules and formulae do not have to be yours—especially when they leave you feeling depressed and inept.

Give yourself some tender, loving care by treating yourself as you would a friend or your favorite pet—not the way your mother treated you. Is it possible that you apply one standard to yourself and a more kindly standard to other people? Don't attack yourself for your anxiety. It needs to be listened to and soothed. You didn't have a nurturing mother so now you must step into that role for yourself.

Become active on your own behalf rather than being a recipient of behavior that diminishes your positive sense of yourself. Plan it so that you can be the one who applies the brakes. Learn to change the topic when your mother gets onto some complaint you do not wish to discuss. If she perpetually criticizes your apartment, arrange to meet her in a restaurant. Experiment in a situation where you do not feel like you are stepping onto a roller coaster with your mother at the controls, as Kimberly, age twenty-seven, explains.

"I have a pair of overalls that my mother cannot stand and one day I wanted to wear them. So, I gathered all my courage and wore them to her house and, before I even walked in the door, I said, 'If you want to talk about them, if you're going to look me up and down all morning, I'll leave right now.' What could she do? She said, 'Come in.'

"I'm also discovering how helpful it is to see her with some humor. My mother hates the fact that I'm in therapy. She thinks it's a waste of money. She put down everything my therapist said. So, my next big step was to announce that we would stop discussing it. A couple of weeks ago, we were driving and I could tell she was dying to ask but didn't want a confrontation. Finally, she coos, 'So, how's your therapist?' She had probably been thinking about how to phrase it fifteen miles back. I told her it was none of her business any more.

"Of course, that wasn't the end of it. I bought a subscription to a lecture series at a Y in my neighborhood and told her about it. After all, this was something she would approve of. It was intellectual, she wouldn't have to worry about me traveling at night, it was inexpensive—only fifty dollars for the series—and maybe she would think I'd meet a guy. She was so pleased that after the first lecture, I called to tell her what a good time I'd had: how interesting it had been and how there'd been a wine and cheese reception afterwards, and how I was really looking forward to the next lecture. I'm trying to include her in my life where she can't do any harm.

"She responds by saying, 'Well, that fifty dollars got you more than any money you paid your therapist!' I had to laugh at the way she will not let it go. Yes, I can laugh now, but it's only because I've made decisions on my own, feel in control, and have achieved some distance."

## Practice Makes Perfect

If a battle with your mother leaves you feeling defeated, instead of sinking into self-hatred and feeling helpless, tell yourself that this is *practice* and that you need time to learn and succeed. If you react to a setback by labeling yourself a failure, you shut down the possibilities for growth. If your parents did not teach you this, you need to develop the capacity for yourself. One of the worst consequences of low self-esteem is that it interferes with your ability to learn.

"I started playing tennis in my twenties," says Rikki, now thirty-six, "and, for the first time in my life, I enjoyed the process of learning something. The game was fun, whether I was tops in it or not. I was not concerned about what others thought and I actually got better. I had never had that experience before.

"As a child, my mother's judgments were so severe, I simply didn't try. The subjects I was good in I could ace.

The ones I wasn't good in, like science and math, I didn't try and didn't care. That made her crazy because I would have a report card that was two-thirds As and then three Ds or an F, which would louse up everything.

"I realize now that I was so aware of her watching me that I could never relax and learn something new. If I didn't get it right on the first try, forget it. If the guy didn't fall for me on the first date, good-bye. I always thought it was because I felt so good about myself but it was exactly the opposite."

It is this shutting-down that is so destructive to the daughter of the Critic. She is afraid to try new things, to meet new people, because the voice in her head is so judgmental. This prevents her from taking in new experiences and new insights that would help her to gain stronger self-esteem.

## Making Peace with the Past

Many daughters find that, as their mothers grow older, as they grow needier and more dependent, their roles reverse. If the daughter is able to learn and change, if she makes a concerted effort to be a better mother to the older woman than her mother was to her, some resolution can be achieved.

"For a while there when my mother was dying," says Rikki, "she was helpless. She had an awful time dying. I guess it was difficult for someone like that to let go of all control, to be incontinent and at the mercy of the people around her. But I had learned to see her as a human being and feel sorry for her and could even tell her that I loved her and feel it."

If you are wrapped up in rage at your mother, look for the significant milestones in her life. Many women become different when their husbands die; the loneliness alters them, their lives are turned upside down, and there might be an opening for you to extricate yourself from the past in a positive way. Instead of sitting in silence, sulking, perpetuating the powerless situation, take some action. You might be able to change your relationship with your mother and thereby change your picture of yourself. You may fear that she is not going to respond but, when she is alone and her need for comfort is more apparent to her and to you, it is up to you to take the risk.

## Strategies for Change

- Respond to "failures" by taking care of yourself. Remember that self-esteem increases or decreases in response to the stresses of life situations, and demands on women in the nineties are high. A particular defeat might shake you up for a while; a failure at work or in love is going to hurt. Better to acknowledge your feelings than to put on a false front. You need to respond to these setbacks by taking care of yourself, comforting yourself, and giving yourself the love and encouragement that your mother failed to.
- Let go of any revenge fantasies. If you are fantasizing revenge for what the world has done to you, if you are thinking about getting back at your parents for every hurt, if you want to trample on others in order to win— you are burying your low opinion of yourself beneath these daydreams. When they collapse, as they are bound to, your self-esteem will be lower than ever.
- Learn to pursue realistic rather than unattainable goals. If you pursue a goal based on fantasy and not related to

your actual talents, capabilities, and opportunities, you are being self-destructive. Self-esteem involves accepting reality and trusting your abilities to pursue a goal that is reachable.

- Stop measuring yourself against others. Strong self-esteem is not a feeling of superiority; it has nothing to do with relishing the fact that you are better than somebody else at anything, no more than it has to do with envying somebody else's looks, achievements, or success. As soon as you start measuring yourself against others you have wandered off the playing field.
- Avoid the dieting issue. In dealing with low self-esteem, poor body image is one trap that's easy to fall into. Society tells us, "Lose ten pounds and you will feel better about yourself!" but many women who look sleek and magnificent still feel they are fat. A lot of them had mothers who had to look perfect. If your mother, who doesn't feel good about her body and is always dieting, sees you as an extension of herself, you are going to have to look perfect, too. Body image is a difficult area in which to start raising your self-esteem.
- Encouragement will come from the strangest corners. Reach out and hang on to any help you get.

"My mother always said that I had a large nose," says Rikki. "She'd tell me, 'You shouldn't wear your hair up because your nose sticks out.' All through high school, I wanted to have a nose job. Then several other girls had nose jobs and they all looked horrible and black and blue and, when I found out what was involved—breaking bones and all—I couldn't go through with it. When I was sixteen or seventeen, I was standing on the street, looking into a bookstore window at a display of a new art book with Botticelli's 'Birth of Venus' on the cover.

Amazingly enough, several people who had also stopped looked at me and said, 'My God, you look just like Botticelli's Venus.' Well, today, I have 'Birth of Venus' toilet paper and a 'Birth of Venus' trash can under my desk. Friends send me postcards from all over the world with pictures of her. She's not ugly and I guess I do look like her so maybe I'm not ugly.

"And I never had a nose job!"

# 8

# The Ostrich

## *The College Student Confronts Feelings*

All through Carla's childhood, her mother's message was "Don't reveal anger or hurt. Just smile." Carla found she couldn't bury her strong feelings.

"I was a volatile kid, cried a lot, had tantrums, ran away— there was never any response from her," says Carla, now forty-one. "My dad came after me, but not Mom. She sent others but that was all. If I had a tantrum on the street that she couldn't avoid, she would bribe me out of it. That's not responding! That's not solving my problem.

"To this day, my mother remembers me as a happy little girl. I remember so much that didn't feel happy. I would get up at night and make sure not to disturb anyone. Nowadays, as a mother, I know when a kid of mine is up. I was anxious and afraid of robbers so I sat in the hall because I couldn't sleep in my room. I must have been pretty young because I couldn't tell time. She didn't want to know I was unhappy. She felt that I shouldn't have unhappy feelings.

"If I tried to tell her, she'd say, 'Why don't you stop it? What's wrong with you anyway?' She couldn't deal with it so she'd walk away—which pretty effectively stops you in your tracks. It felt like a slap in the face.

"If my feelings weren't acceptable that made them all the more scary. Something would happen to frighten me, but I wouldn't actually experience the fear. Of course, I wouldn't tell anybody. It was not permissible to mention such things.

"When I babysat at ten or eleven, I was scared of fires. Who would save me? How would I get the kids out? I used to sit riveted in my seat, not moving until the parents came home. I felt like I was sinking and all I could do was worry, just stare at the clock. Then two days later, I would find myself having a crying jag, not knowing what it was all about.

"I felt closer to my father and, when he went into the hospital when I was twelve, nobody told me why. I wasn't permitted to visit him. Crying wasn't allowed. Mom would say, 'Hide your feelings. Don't impose them on everyone else!' At the funeral, I remember my aunt coming to hug my mother and she pushed her away.

"Afterward, my mother got depressed but she couldn't cry, even when we were alone. Even at that age, I decided I wanted to feel my feelings. That's being alive. My mom was missing a hell of a lot.

"To this day, when she comes to visit, she means well and she'll bring a shopping bag full of barbecued potato chips or cheese doodles—but, if you look, they're past the sales date and, if she really paid attention to what we eat, she'd know not to bring them to our house. As a child, I don't remember big birthday parties. I don't remember nice presents. I got clothes that didn't fit and she would get mad because I wasn't excited. She used to say, 'You're a very cold child.' It wasn't me that was the cold one. She'll come here and say to my kids, 'Well, where's my hug?' but, you know, you've got to work with a kid to get that kind of a response. She doesn't understand that.

"She had no comment when I got married and no comment when I got divorced. I got angry at her once and said, 'You never even asked what the terms of my divorce are!' She's like Jell-O. You cannot make Jell-O sit up and take notice."

## Qualities of the Ostrich

If your mom is an Ostrich, do not go to her for help with a problem. If you are breaking up with or being abused by your partner, she's going to say, "Oh honey, it's just a phase. You can work it out. Go back and talk to him. After all, you look so cute together!" When things go wrong, the Ostrich sticks her head in the sand and simply does not see.

There is little possibility for intimacy here, little honesty about her life or yours. The Ostrich is busy painting rosy pictures and cannot face any unpleasant truths. Of course, this blindness is expressed in terms of her love and concern. She sees herself as devoted to her daughter and, for most of her life, the daughter may believe it.

The Ostrich convinces you that she is the reasonable one and you're crazy. After all, she's always cheery and you are miserable—so you must be at fault.

In the novel *Postcards from the Edge,* Carrie Fisher's roman à clef, Suzanne Vale, in drug rehab, writes in her diary about a visit from her mother:

> I told her I was miserable here, and she said, "Well, you were happy as a child. I can prove it. I have films."[1]

# What's Behind Mom's Behavior?

With a mother like that, you can become a lush, turn to drugs, crash cars, bounce through marriages, and she is never going to notice. Because of her refusal to face her own feelings, she play-acts and needs constant reassurance—and when you demand some attention, her reaction is to grab the spotlight and put it back where it belongs, on her. Others might see her as outgoing and social, you see her as cold and unresponsive.

If you are sullen and depressed and refuse to come out of your room—all the time praying that somebody will offer some solace—the Ostrich will smile and tell people that you're "a deep thinker."

If you're disturbed by nightmares, she'll respond, "It'll pass, honey. Everybody has bad dreams."

If you come home in tears because your friend, Josie, called you fat, she'll say, "You're not fat. It's just a phase you're going through. I never liked that Josie anyway."

---

1. Carrie Fisher, *Postcards from the Edge* (New York: Simon and Schuster, 1987), p. 16.

She sees everything through rose-colored glasses—or doesn't see at all—and you are left in a void. Her denial is an effort to maintain an idealized picture of you, herself, her life, and the world.

## The Healthy Mother and the College Student

When a young woman leaves home to go to college or to get a job, she tries new things, is exposed to new ideas, and lives with a lack of external authority. She is involved in a gentle process of disillusionment about her parents as she learns more about how she is separate from them, what she values in them, and what she can discard. She discovers that living apart from her family, she can still relate, function, and succeed. Once she feels this way about herself, she acknowledges that, at a certain point, to continue blaming her mother for her own limitations is unproductive. The healthy young woman emerges into adulthood with empathy for her mother, ready to assume responsibility for her own life.

However, separating from your mother has two parts: One is seeing her as she really is, the other is presenting yourself as who you really are. This does not mean telling your mother what you might tell your friends. It means something more significant: *showing* her who you are, integrated with who you want to be, demonstrating that you are not a little girl anymore. Once you can do that, you no longer feel like an impostor and she is no longer so firmly implanted in your head.

"I did a real flip when I got to college," says Kelly, in her mid-twenties. "In high school, I was studious and not very social but suddenly I became a butterfly. My grades

dropped . . . not that badly but I went in as a bio major
because my parents wanted me to be a doctor. I couldn't
do it; I barely pulled a C in those classes. For a while I
partied and hung out, skipped classes. My parents
weren't there so I didn't think of their approval or disapproval. It wasn't like I was being this crazy girl; just
school wasn't my priority and I was learning how to live.
No matter how much I party, my values and morals come
from my parents and are never going to change.

"I used to think it was a bad thing if I wasn't the way
my mother wanted me to be and I realized that, while
there is so much of her in me, there are a lot of differences. When I graduated, I was so lost. It was not what
I expected. I thought that everything just fell into place:
you got a good-paying job, you met someone, you married. My parents trained me that you have a career for a
really long time and then you retire. In this day and age,
you could have twenty careers and that's a good thing,
but that's not the way they thought and it clashed with
my life. It took me a long time to realize I am not going
to follow the path my mom wants me to follow. I don't
have that kind of grounded, straight and narrow, pre-
dictable future. Her opinion is important to me but I
can't live by her instructions. I'm not going to have the
life she had or wants me to have and she should be glad.

"At first, I felt guilty because so much happens in
twenty-four hours in college. You come home for
Thanksgiving, that's four days. My mom saw an instan-
taneous different me. I had a whole new group of
friends my parents hadn't even seen. How was I supposed to explain everything that had happened in
the four days of Thanksgiving or even the month I was
home for Christmas?

"She still had a picture of me as her baby who would never do anything wrong. I didn't want to ruin that image. I imagined she would be taken aback by how loose I get with my friends. She'd always say, 'You're so shy, you're so quiet.' 'Mom, you don't know me,' I would say and she'd answer, 'Oh come on, you wouldn't even bat an eyelash in high school. You were painfully shy.' I am shy but I can talk up a storm with anybody and I had to pull it together and say this is who I am. If she doesn't listen or she spits something out that annoys me, I take a deep breath and think, 'I appreciate her opinion and now it's my turn to speak and she's going to have to listen. That was her point of view. Now here's mine!' "

# The Ostrich and the College Student

The daughter of the Ostrich often has a hard time as a college student because she has been taught to hide from her feelings. Not only does she feel a sudden and painful distance from her parents, but she is unable to reconcile who she is with the person they perceive and she has to battle limitations the past has imposed on her.

"My mother was immaculate," says Maryanne, fifty-three. "Coming home from school, the house was perfectly clean, she had her stockings on, her hair was done, her nails were polished, she was reading a book, and dinner was ready. But she would have passed out if I had asked for a hug. I needed hugging, kissing, touching and my mother just couldn't do it. I didn't scream or rave or rant about it. If my mom said wear boots, I wore boots. If she said wear red, I wore red. I'm a pleaser. I don't make waves. I do as I'm told.

"I surprised her once when she was very sick and I came home from college. I opened the door and yelled but there was no answer. I went upstairs and the door was closed but that didn't phase me at the time. She was sitting alone in a rocking chair and she was crying. She got up immediately, 'I'm fine, I'm fine,' she said. 'I didn't expect you.' She hid everything. She had no friends. She didn't talk to my father. I knew she was crying and I knew she was in pain and I knew she was dying but she couldn't share it. I felt for her but I didn't want to be like her.

"In school, I was guarded with my feelings but I was talented at the violin. I played for everything. In ninth grade, I was first violin. I played at the opera. I got all this wonderful praise and it was a place to express myself. But college music majors had to perform a solo two times a year. I liked the exercises and I'm good at them but, when I had to play a solo, I couldn't stand in front of my peers and teachers and let them know who I was.

"One year, I was working on Brahms's Violin Concerto and there are two notes when it starts—D and a B flat, which is a long sustained note that you have to vibrate. Brahms is intense and that B flat was intense and I don't like romantic music anyway. My favorite era is the baroque; everything's in place with perfect cadence, everything resolves. But the Brahms is emotional and my teacher made me play just those two notes for weeks. Then he told me to go out and have an affair and not to come back until I did. I cried for three days, couldn't face my violin teacher, and I never went back to the Brahms. The lack of ability to expose myself was learned from my mom and I was suffering terribly.

"In orchestra, I never liked to sit on the outside where people could stare at me. I always asked the conductor to seat me on the inside. But it was more than that. I was afraid to go to Europe. All my friends went. I had never had a boyfriend and wanted to have one. I never went to doctors because my mother never did. When my mother went shopping, she would not even ask a salesperson for help. It was a declaration of need and she couldn't do that. If she didn't find what she was looking for, we would leave the store.

"I wanted to change but didn't know how until, once, I was in Macy's shopping for a pair of gloves and couldn't find them and thought, 'I'm not going to be like her!' I went to a saleslady and asked. That was the start. Then I did other things; eating alone in a restaurant, reading a book. I loved to conduct. As long as my back was to the audience, I was free. But I had to force myself to turn around and take a bow so I learned to count: bend two three four, up five six. For years I counted to bow because I had to do it if I wanted to have what I loved in my life."

## The Ostrich and Sexuality

The Ostrich is not going to be any help in dealing with your sexuality; chances are that sexual fears are dangerous to her so that she is incapable of responding to yours.

"You couldn't even say the word *sex* to my mom," says Connie, now in her fifties. "You had to spell it. When I got my period, she left a book on my bed. What was the message supposed to be? I thought, 'Why can't we discuss this? Is it so awful? Am I sinful because I'm curious?

Do I have a period because I'm bad? Am I supposed to
feel guilty because boys are responding to me?' If I ever
started really asking any of these questions, my mother
shut me up at once by saying, 'You're still a little girl.'
She refused to notice that I was developing; it never
occurred to her to take me to get a bra. I agonized and
agonized and finally asked for her help. You know what
she did? Gave me the money to get a bra, didn't offer to
go with me. No, not her. Gave me the money and kept
smiling, but what she conveyed was that sexuality was so
dangerous that you cannot acknowledge its presence.
That message stayed with me for years."

The Ostrich's picture of boy–girl relationships is cold
and negative and out of date. She burdens her daughter
with an unreasonably early curfew and nostalgically reflects,
"When I was a girl, we always went out in groups." She
objects to your clothes if they are designed to show off your
figure and dresses herself in shapeless housecoats. When
you try to get her to respond to what you are feeling, she
withdraws. One way or another, she absents herself by
becoming passive and unresponsive or by suddenly talking
nonstop trivia. The Ostrich can chat for hours about what
she is making for dinner while you hold back the tears.

"My mother had one good trait," Connie continues, "her
affability, her outgoingness. Everybody loved her but, as
a mother, she was a factor in my life only in that she
wasn't a factor. She really wasn't *there,* not because she
didn't want to be. I don't think she knew how to be. My
sister was pretty but I was hyperactive, intense, skinny,
wild, and whiny. My mother didn't know what to do with
me. She couldn't get clothes to look nice because I was
so skinny and awkward. She did the things she was

supposed to, went on school trips, came to parent–teacher night, but there was no warmth. Nothing was comfortable.

"I was bright and athletic, the first in my family to go to college, but I never felt feminine and I didn't have sexual feelings until I was in my thirties; my marriage was very repressed sexually. My husband and I were hippies, it was the sixties, and it was good for me because you wore clothing that covered your body—Army–Navy stuff. I could hide; I didn't have to look like a woman and dress up—I was never good at that. Even when I got pregnant the first time, my mother thought it was the immaculate conception.

"With my older daughter, Laila, I was just like my mother; did all the right things, the right nursery, the right friends, the right clothes, but there was no feeling. I was sick for the first three weeks and my mother-in-law lived nearby so she took over. 'You have to do it this way. You have to have this mobile . . .' I never felt that Laila was mine but she was proof to the world that Connie was okay. Relatives, my sister's boyfriends, friends of my parents had always made fun of me, crazy Connie, a little weirdo, always running around. Now I could say, 'See Ma, see Dad. I'm not so crazy.' I'd had sex. I'd produced a normal, healthy, beautiful child.

"I'd never had much experience with real emotion so I didn't know what to feel. I wanted to love Laila, but it was all above the neck. She was a tense child, much like her father, and I always felt that.

"The second one was born when we lived away from her grandparents. I remember thinking, 'Laila was her father's, her grandmother's. Deidre is mine.' She was round and tubby and funny-looking and I didn't care.

I was comfortable with her from the first minute and she was comfortable with me—healthy and happy and terrific. She laughs like me; her personality is like mine.

"It surprised me that I was able to be a good mother, that I felt so sure of myself; maybe it was because nobody was around doing it better. My mother-in-law wasn't leaving me notes, 'Change the diapers three times a day!' With Laila, I was playing dolls and pretending to be a mother, but with Deidre, I was in charge and confident. I had never thought of myself as an imaginative person—I didn't know where I had lost it or why—but I suddenly saw what was missing in my life.

"That's when things began to change. It took years but I started running and getting comfortable with my body and feeling better about myself and sensing these feelings and didn't know what it was all about. Men were looking at me—and I liked it. All of a sudden, finally, at thirty, that long history of sexual repression exploded. My husband was not responding. Our lives were going in different directions. He was into pot smoking but I never wanted to be a hippie. I had just been pretending all those years. I tried, suggested counseling, wanted him to go to tennis parties with me. He said no. He knew something was wrong but was willing to put up with it for the sake of the kids. By doing nothing!

"I was married, had two children, but I was like a sixteen year old and didn't do rational things. It tore everything apart. If I could have handled it differently, I would have, but the volcano exploded and I thought, 'Wow! So this is what it's all about!'

"I started going out with other men and then I met Hank. He was in his twenties, a ski bum—but this guy loved me! He thought I was beautiful. He thought I was sexy. I had such intense feelings for the first time in my life. And the sex! I used to go to his apartment in the afternoons. He would call and I would get a baby-sitter and run. He had this tiny room and roommates so there was often somebody there and we had to control how much noise we made. But the drama, the tension, the clenched teeth, and the shame—they all made the sex more exciting. I remember thinking that the walls were going to explode. I would do anything for him, go anywhere. I figured it would calm down, it would end—it didn't. But he was irresponsible and undependable. He would promise to call and then wouldn't—and I would be afraid to wash the dishes in case I missed the ring of the phone with the water running!

"Finally, I ran off with him to the Virgin Islands. I grabbed both girls but Laila put up a big fight, screaming and everything, so I left her. Deidre was three and went with us but Hank was volatile, things were not right for her there so, eventually, I sent her home.

"Of course, I was guilty and worried. Hank didn't seem to understand. If he was feeling good, he'd never notice that I was washed out and feeling bad. Then I'd pull away and that set off a down mood in him, so he'd blame me. He was so intense, I felt engulfed. He turned into a control freak. When we were decorating our apartment, he either rejected my ideas or took them as his. Eventually, he said that he didn't want me involved. I kept trying to laugh it off. We were behaving just like my mother and father!

"One day, it was so silly, the place was being painted and I had cleared two rooms for the painter and went to relax and watch T.V. I told Hank that I'd do the plants the next day. But no, he just had to do it all, it had to be his way, he was always in charge. So he did it but I knew he resented that I wasn't helping. Nobody had been saying what they felt and that battle turned into something ugly and that was the time he started to hit. And that was when I got out.

"I came back in a bad state and had to face divorce proceedings. There was a difficult custody fight and the girls had to get up in court and tell the judge that they wanted to stay with their father. Laila led the way and I guess Deidre followed—but who could blame either one?

"I was shattered. My life was in ruins. Everyone turned away from me, including myself. I couldn't explain what had happened to anyone and it would take me years to figure it out but there was no undoing what had been done."

## What's in Store for the Ostrich's Daughter?

One of the great dangers of having an Ostrich for a mother is that you will choose somebody like her—cold, unfeeling, unresponsive—for a mate. You hope to change him into what you dreamed of having as a child: a loving, embracing, open, and available mother. It won't work.

Or you might fall for somebody who goes to the other extreme—some guy who appears to be highly charged and overemotional—because you have been so blocked in expressing yourself. You think he is supplying you with feelings where they have been lacking; then you discover he is actually as unresponsive as she was.

This is one of the most serious residues of life with an Ostrich. If you do not face your despair and rage at not having your infantile needs met, they will linger below the surface and infect all your intimate relationships. You tell yourself that if only you were better, if only you were smarter, if only you were more loving—your partner would come through, just as you believed as a child that, if only you could do things Mom's way, you would be loved. Under this oppressive desire to please are other feelings left over from your childhood: You resented the fact that she did not get gratification from who you really were and what you really felt. You suspected that she wanted you to fit some image that had nothing to do with you. You pretended that her coldness did not bother you, but it always did.

If we haven't learned to work through our childhood traumas, we create situations in our adult lives that are replicas of our childhoods just to see if, this time, we can get our needs met. We're not conscious of what we are doing; not until it is too late and we are left with egg on our faces—yet again.

When something changes our internal balance—whether positive or negative—it makes us anxious and may push us into impulsive behavior. Instead of dealing with our feelings, instead of confronting them, action promises an end to the anxiety. If the first glimmer of a feeling brings with it the threat of rejection, we rush to find the rejection because the tension of waiting for the other shoe to drop is greater than the actuality could ever be. We seek out familiar situations, familiar relationships because there we feel safe.

If you feel worthless and stupid, you'll behave in a way that confirms these feelings. If you feel deserving of punishment, you do something that assures you'll be punished.

When the birth of her second child opened Connie up to her sensual being, it led to an eruption of emotions that she found difficult to contain. Since she felt that sexuality was bad, her first impulses caused her to behave in such a way as to bring the wrath of her family and society down upon her. Allowing herself to learn about those impulses, to feel safe with them, would have required that she live for a while with forbidden impulses without acting on them. She needed to work her way through these taboos in order to figure out what was happening.

# Separation: Acknowledging Your Feelings

The process of growing, changing, and self-discovery is scary—much as it was in adolescence. If you had a mother who did not allow you to express what you were feeling, who refused to respond, who made you feel ashamed and guilty, you are going to be prone to act out whenever you find yourself in a similar situation.

Women without a strong sense of self are particularly vulnerable to emotional injury—rejection, criticism, slights that would be minor to anyone else. A strong sense of self protects us against such hurt. Women with inner strength can fall in love—can connect with someone physically and emotionally—without needing to sit beside the telephone waiting for it to ring.

If you feel demolished every time you fail to get a raise or a promotion, if you are devastated when you don't get an invitation to that special party, recognize that your responses are coming from the past. If Connie had taken the time to deal with her feelings, to experience them, she might not have married the first time, might not have judged herself so harshly after her first child was born, might not have allowed the explosion of her sexuality to overwhelm her life. Pain, hurt, even joy can set off the eruption if you have had no training in how to deal with emotion.

Change requires action as well as talk and analysis. Sometimes you have to force yourself to do something that you have avoided—as Maryanne did by asking for help in the department store. Until you realize that nothing terrible will happen, you are likely to experience discomfort but, if you keep practicing, the strangeness and self-consciousness will disappear.

When trying to change, find a relatively safe environment, one in which the risks are minor. You can build up a sense of yourself as capable of major change once you have experimented with small ones.

If your assumption is that, by asserting yourself, you will be rejected, try out an assertion with someone you like and note the results; your anxiety, the way you dealt with it, what her reaction was. For instance, the next time your friend assumes you will pick up theater tickets for both of you, tell her your schedule is tight instead of twisting yourself into knots trying to please her. Identify, observe, and evaluate your behavior. Check with friends to determine to what degree your conclusions are valid—or whether you are still reading reality according to learned responses from childhood.

By thinking about what awaits you, what you will do, and how you will feel afterward, you can handle new experiences without being at the mercy of the moment. And, after mastering the first skill, it will be easier to go on to the next.

Zoe, thirty, is a stand-up comic who had been playing the smaller clubs around the country and thought that her big break had come. She was up for a spot on cable T.V., which would have given her national exposure. "The first audition went really well," she says, "and they kept calling me back, a terrific sign. When I didn't get it, I crawled into bed and stayed there for days—eating, watching talk shows, trying to sleep. The strange thing was I didn't cry until one night on *60 Minutes* there was this piece about mentally ill people being comforted by cats and the tears were streaming down my face! And that was the start of my coming out of it. Those tears and the recognition that I needed somebody—even a cat!—to hang out with and be blue."

What Zoe discovered was that the first step in recovering from pain is allowing yourself to mourn. Dr. Audrey Amdursky says, "Such a loss may feel like the end of the world and it is the end of whatever you wanted. You have to allow yourself a period of experiencing that. You may feel at a loss to go on. However, you will go on."

# Strategies for Change

- Realize that clinging to Mom is a way of avoiding frightening feelings. Once you embark on the process of separation, once you turn your back on your old ways of dealing with anxiety, you come face to face with a scary black hole. You have three options: You can turn back to Mom and retreat. You can act out, which is simply another way of avoiding your feelings. Or you can dig deep into the hole and find out what is buried. In order to fully separate, decide to dig!
- Mourn your childhood. As you grow more aware of the feelings you have squashed and notice how severely you treat yourself—like being excessively self-critical or unforgiving of your own mistakes—you'll need to recognize the undermining climate in which you grew up and how you pretzeled yourself into acceptable shapes. Then you

have to mourn the tenderness and responsiveness you were not given.

- Denying your pain never helps. "Eating soothes for the moment," says Dr. Amdursky. "It lets you forget. Sugar creates a little high so you get over some of the doldrums but it doesn't erase the fact of the loss so you end up feeling worse. If you don't eat, you are going to have these horrible feelings, which you will have to tolerate. Eventually, they will pass."

- Be prepared for your reactions to a crisis. The healthy mother provides you with a loving sense of the world and your value in it, a sense that will get you through every crisis. If your mom was not there for you, as is the case for the daughter of the Ostrich, every crisis will threaten you with fear of her abandonment. As a child, you had a right to feel deprived, to feel unprotected, to feel scared. But that was long ago. If you don't stop and take a look at such feelings when they bubble up in the present, you will be tempted to reach for the first pair of arms that remind you of hers, which reassure you that she will not vanish. No one can provide the security you seek. You have to find it inside yourself.

- Every time you experience tension or anxiety, ask yourself what is going on, what has upset you, and why. Once you identify the source of your upset, you will have less of a need to run. What felt overwhelming to you as a child (when it is reevaluated in the present) may not be such a big deal. When you are trying to change an old pattern—or one is being changed despite your wishes—ask yourself what frightens you. Achieving self-understanding increases your capacity for self-control and diminishes your vague fears regarding feelings. Everyone has to learn to accept and tolerate a certain amount of anxiety and tension in life. Similarly, you have to learn to accept feelings of resentment and hostility. By figuring out what is causing these, by allowing yourself to feel them if they are justified, you will be able to express them in proportion to the situation.

- Fear is not love. You were not responsible for what happened to you as a child—but you are responsible for the present. Stop believing that if only you behave differently, that if only you are closer to what your mother or your lover wants, then she or he will love you forever. This is fear, not love, and you have created it to fulfill needs that were not met in childhood. Only by bringing these old needs out of the shadows can you decide whether your behavior accomplishes what it is supposed to. But you cannot do that if you are continually getting trapped in the past.
- Face the painful truth. Facing the fact that you were harmed as a child is painful. But only by accepting this truth will you be able to see yourself through eyes different than those of your mother. Only then will you stop seeking the maternal validation of which you were deprived and only then will you find some peace. Reality can be painful but unless you force yourself to look at it, you'll find yourself simply going from one illusion to another.

# 9

# The Competitor
## The Working Woman Starts a Life of Her Own

**W**hen Liza Minnelli was just starting out in show business, her mother, superstar Judy Garland, said to a reporter about Liza and her sister, Lorna: "Liza is already on her way and if that's what she wants, super. Lorna, however, has a much better voice than Liza and will probably overtake her if she decides to get into the business."[1]

## Qualities of the Competitor

The Competitor comes in various subcategories. The first is the out-and-out lioness who growls the minute you step on

---

1. James Spada, *Judy & Liza* (New York: Doubleday, 1983), p. 94.

her turf. There is no subtlety, no disguise, no pretense; she is out for the kill and armed. She will put you down—in private and, even worse, in public. She will set father against daughter, sister against sister, when her supremacy is threatened.

Picture eighteen-year-old Minnelli, trying to get a career off the ground, eager to prove herself in a world where everybody idolized her mother—and imagine what it felt like to read that remark in the papers. How could she possibly have understood that behind such a statement was not viciousness, but fear?

Another type of Competitor is not so direct; the growl is covered by a pretty smile, a giggle. Everybody loves her. Nobody but you senses that the fangs are bared.

"Whenever anybody came by," says Erica, thirty-eight, "the postman, the UPS guy, friends from school, a date of mine—Mom would turn on the charm. And the trouble was she could always outshine me. After all, she had so many more years of practice. If someone was talking to me, she would keep interrupting. If I tried to tell a story, she would say, 'No, the way it happened was this....' She wasn't doing it to put me down, but she was desperate for affection and attention.

"My dad was older and not much of a husband. So my mom used every situation to satisfy her own needs. Okay, I can understand that. What I can't forgive is that she was so insensitive to my needs. I was the kid, not she! The awful part was that I began to believe that it would always be more fun if she were there; the way she kept the conversation going, she was always the life of the party. But she destroyed my self-esteem and it wasn't until I got away from her that I was able to recoup and rebuild."

Perhaps the most devious type of Competitor is the romantic. She creates a fairy-tale image of what she was like as a girl and fills you with stories about how exceptional she was, how great the possibilities before her were. Of course, you do not know if this is true or not, but the stories are enchanting; it's like having a real-life princess in your house. The problem is that you cannot test your own abilities against this fantasy figure; she is always going to come out on top and you are always going to feel like a failure.

To compound the damage, the Competitor bemoans the fact that life didn't turn out the way it should have—usually blaming your father—and expecting you to comfort her for the loss. Thus any success you might have causes double trouble; it challenges her position as the best and the brightest and threatens her with loss of the consolation she has found for not living up to her dreams.

"My mother was the most beautiful woman in Brookline of her era, which I've heard from her—many times," says forty-nine-year-old Rosemary with a trace of humor, "and I totally believe it. I've got a picture of her when she was twenty-three. She was an exquisite woman who had the brains and foresight to go to law school. Life should have been rosy, but she made the mistake of marrying the man who was number one in their class, a brilliant guy who made a terrible husband. He was one of those superficial charmers who, underneath, have no feeling for people at all. Besides, he was a philanderer who ended up making passes at my college roommates! She started with everything in the world and the expectation that she would continue to be worshipped for her beauty and brains and career—and she was let down in her major relationship.

"She turned extremely bitter. Three years before she had me, she had a miscarriage. Then I was born and she never went back to law. For the rest of her life—forty plus years—she had no career, no direction, just this lousy relationship as her major focus. As a result, she demanded absolute loyalty from the two most important women in her life—me and her sister. My aunt has been married for fifty-four years; by the time my mother died I had been married nineteen years. Each of the closest women in her life had decent marriages with men who cared about them. And that really pissed her off!"

Rosemary laughs, but her laughter fades quickly.

"Her life was empty. She had no career and was very smart. That was the saddest part, how smart she was. She could have been anything. As a kid, she played the piano so well that she could have made a career out of that. This talented woman ended with a life that was totally empty. I don't know what my mother did with her days. I know that at one o'clock her housekeeper came. She didn't go out before that so her day didn't begin until probably two o'clock in the afternoon. What she did, I cannot picture. Did she have lunch with friends? Did she go shopping? She always dressed beautifully but I cannot picture my mother in a department store."

How can you measure yourself against a ghost? How can you try to be better than she was at anything? How can you dream of succeeding when she could have, should have, would have been the most incredible . . . if only things had been different?

Most Competitors are multitalented. The lioness can turn on the charm; the romantic can turn vicious. The result is the same. Their ultimate message is: "You may not outshine me and you may not leave me."

However, even a first-class competitive mother like Judy Garland can be handled if her daughter keeps one eye on what she wants and another on the reality of her mother's demands.

In the biography, *Judy & Liza,* author James Spada tells about the night Liza Minnelli was opening in her first starring role in a touring musical. The show had begun and the backstage telephone rang. The stage manager was alarmed; it should not have been ringing except in dire emergency because it could be heard by the audience.

He picked up the phone quickly. The call was for Liza and the stage manager explained that she was on stage. The caller asked that a message be left: Judy Garland had just tried to commit suicide.

The stage manager decided to wait to tell Liza until after the performance was over but, at intermission, the phone rang again. This time, Liza picked it up. "Is she going to be okay?" she was heard to say. The answer was evidently positive. "Tell her I'll see her after the show," Liza said.

Then she went out and gave a terrific second act performance.

## What's Behind Mom's Behavior?

Think about where your mom grew up, in what kind of an environment, within what culture. Was she raised when assertive women were labeled as "masculine"? Women of earlier generations had difficult times struggling against the passivity and compliance expected of them and the authoritativeness they needed in order to run their homes. They were confused themselves and, out of the fear and shame and sense of inadequacy, many of them became Competitors.

"My mother was not close to her mother," says Eileen, twenty-two. "We often heard that nobody liked Grandma, even Mommy. I remember that we never had liquor in the house but, when Grandma came, we had to get a bottle of whiskey and it went upstairs to her bed-room, never to be seen again.

"I don't think my grandmother was happy in her marriage. I heard it from cousins, the family, but, still, she would ask me all the time, 'Do you have a boyfriend?' She believed that you needed a man to be worthwhile and my mom had no other options. My grandmother said, 'You're getting married,' and that was it.

"My mom knows that she gave up a lot by treating my father the way she did. She never said, 'Could you vacuum today? Could you do the laundry?' and she knows that I will. I have to work. I have to get a job. I want to succeed. I made a conscious effort to have a huge circle of friends like my mother never had. But there is jealousy between the generations and always has been.

"My grandparents had a place on Lake George and my mom's whole desire in life was for her and my dad to get a place there also. Once they had, one night, I woke up and found my mother weeping because her mother had made her feel so guilty. Grandma had attacked my mom because it had been so 'easy' for my parents. My dad had a good job.

They had nice cars. And it had been so hard for Grandma."

## The Healthy Mother and the Young Working Woman

One of a mother's jobs is to let her daughter know that she is good at things, maybe better than her mother is—that her opportunities are endless, that her mother would be pleased if her daughter went further than she did in life.

A mother should encourage her daughter to see the world, to aim high, to explore and experiment, to make friends, to grow comfortable and successful in life. She should not be threatened every time you take a step toward the door, she should not resent it if you succeed where she failed, she should not be trying with all her might to keep you within the tight confines of her own life.

> "I have a running gag with my four year old," says Chloe, who is approaching thirty. "It concerns that silly song from *The Lion King*—'Aki Mama Tata'—or whatever it is. I can't even remember the title and she knows the song by heart. Every time I sing it, she howls with glee. She gets such a kick out of the fact that she can remember it and I can't. It dawned on me the other day that what she enjoys is the sensation that she does something better than I do. She has a better memory than I have—we've talked about that often—and that sense of besting me gives her great pleasure."
>
> In a similar vein, Rhoda, fifty, explains how, despite her own eventual success at college, she did not do as well as a freshman as her daughter did. "And I even went to the closet and dragged out old transcripts to prove it to her!" Rhoda exclaims.

# The Competitor and the Young Working Woman

When Rhoda talks about her own mother, she's less amused: "She claimed she didn't want me thinking I was perfect so, way back when I was three, four years old, she'd be on the phone and, if she had something nice to say about me, she'd talk about 'R'—so I wouldn't know. If I ever offered to clean up, she'd say, 'You're offering to clean up? I can't believe it.' Once I was on some committee at school, and she said, 'I can't believe you're working so hard. I never saw you do this. What are you, sick?' She loved it that I was a scared, shy kid. She liked the fact that I didn't run off with my friends and leave her. The only praise I got was, 'Isn't she wonderful? Look at how nice and quiet she is.'"

The Competitor has trouble with your marrying well or being successful at work. She dresses too young, flirts with your boyfriend, and flinches when she finds out that you got a promotion. She would never admit it, but she is downright jealous!

How can you establish an independent existence when your mother has for so long silently—and sometimes not so silently—communicated that to leave her is to destroy her, to outshine her is to crush her? On the one hand, you are expected to fulfill your mother's thwarted longings. On the other, you know that any success arouses your mother's envy. You sense the hostility, the danger in a woman so frustrated and unhappy. So you fear the most awful retaliation.

A child. when faced with such feelings, turns the danger inward. By renouncing her self, by forsaking any possibilities for her own success, the daughter preserves the security of her childhood. She is so scared of her mother that she may not even allow herself to wish to escape. Often, this daughter, as a young adult, finds herself prone to depression.

> "When I went away to college," says Nell, now fifty, "I saw myself as abandoning my mother, so anxiety and guilt made me a mental wreck. I fell into a yearlong depression until I met my husband; we married when we graduated. It seemed the only way out. He was a teacher so I became one, too. I remember when I was in sixth grade, saying to myself that whatever I became in life, I didn't want to teach. It seemed so boring! But it was the best job I could have to maintain a family and raise kids and keep my husband, so that's the way it turned out."

Depression often occurs when the daughter of the Competitor is in a new place in life, when options present themselves. She becomes frightened of opportunities, which mean giving up the old, safe limits to her life. So she pulls back and refuses to follow a new path by paralyzing herself with depression.

The alternative to depression is not the absence of all pain but the freedom to express her feelings. These feelings will not only be cheerful, happy, and good—they can also include rage, jealousy, envy, aggression, hunger, and even greed—all of which a daughter is forced to bury if she has spent years being her mother's supplicant.

## What's in Store for the Competitor's Daughter?

Even if the child of a Competitor beats the odds and does well at school, any success brings with it the possibility—

and maybe even the requirement—that she leave Mom's embrace. So this girl is obliged to remain unsuccessful. Success threatens the structure of the mother–daughter relationship. Success implies the humiliation of Mom. No matter how much the daughter achieves in life, no matter what strengths she acquires—she still refuses to take the power from her mother.

Nell continues: "After I married and had my own life, my mother was constantly criticizing me. She told everybody how awful I was. We would stop talking for six months at a time, then one or the other of us would reach out through an intermediary. It was so uncomfortable not to talk to her; it wasn't that you could not talk to her and forget about her—you didn't talk to her and you thought about her all the time! My father would call and say, 'I can't live with your mother while you're not talking to her.' I would get calls from second cousins and friends: 'It's awkward to have to say this, Nellie, but, you know, you're really not paying enough attention to your mother. You're not treating her right.' So, I would try—and then she would get mean again because she wanted to be the focus of my life and the fact that I had a husband and a daughter and a job all infuriated her further.

"My mother turned into a major drinker when she got older because she was so frustrated and unhappy. She would start on the Scotch at five in the afternoon and get meaner as she drank—I would just sit there and take it and grow more and more scared. Once I asked my father, 'Do you think when she drinks she could take a knife and come after me?' I was that afraid of her. My parents were very well off and, after my father died, I was afraid that she would cut me off without a cent—which she threatened to do many times.

"Before he died, I said to him, 'How could you leave everything to Mom? You know how sick she is. You see how she treats me!' and he answered, 'I've given her so much grief during her life, I couldn't take half of everything away, even to give it to you.' I should have stood up and screamed, '*Yes, you can!*' but I didn't. It wasn't really a fear of violence, or a fear that she would leave the money to somebody else. There was simply no way I could walk away."

What does a woman like Nell do? She turns herself into a caregiver, the woman behind the power. She muffles her own aggression and ambition. Due to her lack of experience with these feelings, she cannot tell the difference between assertion and hostility—and that scares her. She avoids the guilt of competitive feelings by remaining dependent on her mother. She is comfortable as second fiddle—not because she is afraid of failing, but because she is afraid of success. At work, she might be a better administrator than her boss but she does not dare act on that belief. Why? As a child, she was afraid that if she ever became too independent, her mother would decide that she could make it on her own and abandon her. Thus, as an adult, with lovers and husbands and bosses, she presents herself as powerless.

"She controlled my life. All I wanted was to get away from her and I thought the only way was to get married," Nell explains. "Now, as I watch my daughter, who is turning twenty-four, all I can do is pray, 'Don't let her grab an unsuitable guy on some theory that you have to get married at a certain age.' I don't mean to say that my husband is an unsuitable guy—I would not say that.

I would say that if I hadn't been so desperate to get away . . . I don't even know how to finish this sentence.

"We have a good marriage, twenty-nine years' worth. We are not at all alike. Kindness and gentleness are very important to me. He's just the opposite. He doesn't hear so well these days so the criticisms he used to bark at me are now so loud that it drives me nuts because I like peace and quiet. I try to be sympathetic; losing your hearing is tragic but it's nothing to get angry about. But I would say that if I hadn't been so eager to get away from my mother, I might have taken a little longer to choose who I married. It is possible that I could have found somebody that I would have been more like . . ."

## *Fear of Assertion*

In a male-dominated society, girls are rewarded for being "good," for not making waves, for not competing. Reticence and a lack of self-sufficiency have for too long been seen as signs of femininity. Women have been pushed into the roles of accommodators, mediators, adapters, and empathizers. From the time they are toddlers they are told that their main goal in life is to serve others—first by being a good daughter, then a good wife, then a good mother.

Initiating conflict has never been seen as a womanly characteristic in our society. Standing up for yourself (when done by a female) is interpreted as depriving someone else of their rights or as hurting them. Women who have been brought up this way have an especially difficult time expressing anger—or anything approaching anger. But assertion is not anger. Ambition is not anger. However, you may confuse these with anger if your mother was a woman who was angry at her own frustrations in life, or at anyone doing better than she did.

## Fear of Competition

Female athletes learn that competitiveness has nothing to do with anger. You want to beat someone, you want to be the best there is, you want to top your own record—and this is a pleasurable, exciting feeling that has no tinge of anger. Women tennis champs who are best friends and doubles partners, when facing one another in a singles match, play with no holds barred.

Men may be deficient in the nurturing, caring impulses that women are encouraged to feel—but when it comes to standing up for themselves and fighting for the recognition they deserve, these impulses in males are approved from the cradle. In the perfect world of the feminist future, men will teach women what they do best and women will teach men what they do best.

Certainly, young women of today who are encouraged to get involved in sports, who have role models like runner Jackie Joyner-Kersee and tennis champ Steffi Graff—who are fiercely competitive, tops at what they do, and proud of it—are going to have an easier time with competition. They fight to develop their talents, they want to use them, and they demand to be rewarded. No one today would find anything wrong with that—except for a competitive mother who does not wish to relinquish her throne.

Thus the daughter of the Competitor does not allow herself the capacity for independent behavior. She is likely to seek false protection from a man. Because she is looking to replace the mother she never left, she finds a guy who treats her like a child. She believes that she cannot make it on her own; she changes her identity only from being somebody's daughter to being somebody's wife. She may move directly from her mother's home to her husband's so that she never gets any experience living alone and fears not being able to survive it.

"Love" comes to mean being taken care of—not being encouraged, not being admired, not being challenged, and certainly not a relationship between two independent equals. Eventually, the husband may get bored and drift away. The wife sees him as cold and unloving. She feels even more powerless and is right back where she started.

# Separation: Finding a Mentor

Replacing Mom with a mentor—someone you admire because you feel that she's smarter, stronger, and more independent than you are and someone who can help you develop a better opinion of yourself—is a tool you can use in adulthood if you did not avail yourself of it as a teen. This mentor, or mother surrogate, can help you separate from your mother by supplying a set of standards different from hers.

Since women have begun to see the universality of their problems in the workplace, since they have learned about networking and helping one another, the mentoring relationship between an older woman and a younger one has become more accepted and encouraged.

A mentor can be of value because she is different from your mom, because she gives you a chance to emulate other qualities and new values. A mentor who is like your mother can also be valuable. Because she has less power over you than your mother, because the entanglement is less intense, you may be able to deal with traits in her that were disabling to you in your mother. Because you are more separate from her, because you are not so vulnerable, because she is less threatening and less threatened, she feels less toxic. In the space created by those significant differences you may learn to deal with this surrogate in a new way.

Gail, twenty-five, is an elementary school teacher in
Winston-Salem, North Carolina. She tells this story:
"I was hired to teach sixth grade in a school with a team-
teaching philosophy. There were two other teachers on
my team and they had a strong say in the hiring process.
To tell you the truth, I was amazed that they had picked
me. One was an older guy, near retirement, and the
other was an uptight woman in a tailored suit, Pamela,
who reminded me of my mother.

"There I was, wearing white socks and Birkenstocks
for the interview, determined to be myself. I was not
going to play a role so I gave it to them straight; my
desire to be a creative teacher, my belief in honesty in
the classroom, my hope for student involvement—the
whole radical new approach.

"Later, I asked Pamela why they had okayed me and
she said that Ben, the older guy, and she did see how
straitlaced and traditional they were and felt they
needed someone like me to balance the team. I was
flattered and reassured and began to like her so, when
she started giving me advice, I could listen—like about
keeping my mouth shut in the lunchroom and smiling
when some jerk of a teacher was saying something
ridiculous. I had never played politics before, I'd always
led with my chin and taken pride in my rebelliousness,
and I'd always gotten into trouble. With Pamela, I could
learn.

"I could see how competitive she was with other
teachers—how she talked too much and demanded the
spotlight all the time, exactly like my mom. But I could
also see her vulnerability, her insecurity. She needed me
as an audience and with Pamela it didn't make me feel
put down. She needs center stage because she's anxious

and deals with her anxiety by talking. I could mediate for her with other people who found her self-centered. I protected her and defended her because I didn't see her as so powerful.

"I was able to use her to learn to enter the system and be more successful. I did admire the way she managed things and she was, in her way, a good teacher. But acknowledging her good qualities did not make me feel lesser. She laughed at me because I was the oddball on the team; I laughed at her because she was so uptight. It was a lovely relationship because neither of us was threatened by the other.

"I had devised this terrific math project for my kids. They had to create a scrapbook illustrating how they would spend a million dollars. They were to clip ads out of the papers, figure out the taxes on the prices, buy no more than twenty items, and come within one dollar of the million. They were thrilled, I was thrilled, we all had a ball, and everyone learned a lot.

"On Open School Night, the mother of one of my kids runs up to Pamela and starts gushing about how wonderful I was and how much her daughter loved me and all about the million-dollar project. And dear old Pamela says to the mother, 'Yeah, but do they know their multiplication tables?'

"Of course the kid reports this to me and you know what I do? I say, 'Don't worry, you'll know them,' and we both have a good laugh on Pamela. I could actually laugh! I didn't feel hurt or deflated or inadequate. I didn't feel the need to defend myself as I do with my mother. Tears did not rush to my eyes. I can't tell you how pleased I was with myself!"

# Strategies for Change

- Realize what you have invested in remaining powerless. As the daughter of a competitive mother, you may be terrified to face your ability to change things. Perhaps you are convinced that, if you become self-sufficient, if you stand up for what you want, you will lose the only identity you have ever known—after all, you would no longer be somebody's other. Remaining powerless helps you to hide your anger.
- Know that you don't have to be a victim. Because of the intimacy and intensity of the mother–daughter relationship, competitive moms have a lot of power. With a competitive mother, her love for you is unconditional only if she wins. Don't buy into it!
- Learn to open up to others, perhaps to a therapist. In order to break out of this no-win relationship with your mother and allow other experiences in, it is necessary to overcome your feelings of shame and humiliation. The first courageous step is to open up to others so that they can help you. You might discover that not everybody responds to you the way your mom did. Alternate views and ways of behaving might enter your life and affect your thinking. The success of this endeavor might enable you to go one step further and dig beneath the surface so that you start to experience your feelings instead of muffling them.
- Find friends to talk to. They will help you get some distance, distinguish your feelings from the reality, and see things with more objectivity. This is one of the secrets of the success of support groups: Alcoholics Anonymous and its offshoots, self-help discussions, study classes. It is often the bonding with others that offers a way out of the problem.

- Cultivate a best friend or a mentor. Most young women learn in adolescence that a best friend can help to satisfy the longings for closeness with Mother when separating from her is a compelling task. Sharing tales about your mother with a girlfriend will help you to compare experiences and get a better hold on the reality of life with your mother. Your friend's take on your mother can enable you to dispel the myths about her. You can learn to laugh at her the way your friends do.

  Begin your search for a new identity for yourself based on this revised view of Mom, on the attractive qualities you see in your friends' moms, and on other female figures whom you admire. Sharing your aspirations with women who are not jealous enables you to be less afraid of asserting yourself. Developing friendships is not only a way of relieving the tensions in the mother–daughter relationship, it becomes a way out of the entanglement.

- Take the risk. Without finding someone to talk to, without reexperiencing what you should have found in adolescence, you cannot begin the journey. It might be too frightening and complex to deal head-on with your mother; friends are less powerful and so the danger is less, allowing you to maintain some control and objectivity. By improving your capacity to trust friends, by giving up unrealistic expectations of them, by becoming more patient, by learning to compromise, by daring to reveal yourself—you are solving the problems created by the relationship you have had with your mother.

# 10

# The Guilt-Monger
## The Daughter
## Enters Adulthood

*L*ast year, Doreen, age twenty-nine, charged an expensive ticket and battled lines at the airport to fly home to visit her parents at Thanksgiving. When she finally arrived at the house, it wasn't exactly filled with holiday cheer.

"The lights were dim, the table wasn't set, my mother was in bed with a migraine," Doreen explains. "My father had already started sipping on the booze. I knew my mother expected me to come upstairs, sit by her bed, apply cold compresses, and soothe her in a darkened room. Is this why I flew all the way home? Not to mention that this happens whenever I visit. But this time I refused to give in. I loaded Dad in the car, went and bought a pre-cooked turkey, canned cranberry sauce, instant mashed potatoes—it wasn't gourmet cooking but it was fast. In half an hour, I called up the stairs, 'Mom, dinner is on the table. You'd better come down.' Of course, she did. What else could she do?"

# Qualities of the Guilt-Monger

You take her to Florida, she asks, "Why not the Caribbean?" You spend an afternoon at her hospital bed, she asks, "Aren't you coming tonight?" She clings to her deprivations.

Jackie, forty-two, says, "It's been thirty years since my father deserted us; the phone bill is still in his name. When my kid sister got engaged, Mom's first words were, 'Who's going to walk you down the aisle?' No joy. No pleasure. No hug. Every time she talked about the wedding, it was, 'Who's going to walk her down the aisle?' The whole event was centered on her deprivation.

"To this day, she'll call me up and say, 'I hate to bother you, but the phone is not working, the vacuum cleaner's broken ...' I go over there. Of course, it's something stupid like push this button on the phone, take the rubber thing in the vacuum and suck it up. She gets in the car and can't close the door. 'Ma,' I say, 'I'm going to drive away now. The door has to be closed.' She tries but, you know, car doors have to be slammed and, eventually, I get out, go around, do it for her. She always makes sure that everybody knows they are obligated to take care of her."

The Guilt-Monger claims that she is lonely and ignored, yet the world circles around her needs. She claims that she is helpless, yet she wields incredible clout. She is supposedly interested only in you but if you come to her with a problem, it will cause her heart palpitations and you'll end up taking her to the emergency room. She is always putting herself down, always seeking sympathy, and always denying that she is doing it.

"It was the last straw," says thirty-six-year-old Heather, "when I told my mother that I was divorcing Kevin—not an easy moment for me. She took it terribly. She started to cry and ramble on: 'How could it be any different? You had such an awful example as you were growing up. Your dad was terrible: I only stayed for the good of you kids and what does it bring me but heartache . . . and now this!'

"I'm wondering when she's going to say something comforting and she finally blurts out, 'If you leave Kevin, what else can I do? I'm going to leave your dad!' She bursts into tears of agony and reaches for me to console her! It was the work of a genius! In three minutes, she had completely switched the focus from my pain to hers and gypped me out of everything I needed. Not only does she steal all the attention and sympathy—she steals my feelings, too!"

## What's Behind Mom's Behavior?

"Even at age twenty-three, living away from home, I'm constantly filled with guilt," says Teresa. "I went out last night and, if my mom had called this morning and said nothing more than, 'You sound a little hoarse,' guilt would have raged through my body. If I'm visiting them and I get home at three in the morning, I still take off my shoes and creep upstairs. When I wake up, I don't care if I feel like crap or not, I make sure to bounce out of bed and head downstairs with a perky, 'Hi, Mom!' I have this guilt that I had fun and that she was worrying about me and I worry about her worrying about me.

"There's no question that me and my brother were her whole life. We were what she did. She had no female friends. I don't think that she and my dad have gone to a movie since 1970. She doesn't seem to have a problem with that. Every single fight that my parents had stemmed from the two of us.

"They never fought about what was going on between them, except once, when I was in fourth grade, I heard something during an argument I'll never forget. My mother screamed, 'If you want to have sex with someone else, you go ahead!' and from that time on I always knew there was an emptiness in her life."

It is crucial that a young girl see her mother as being relatively content: that she has chosen her role, succeeds in it, is not deprived. The mother who is desperately unhappy or depressed, who is suffering in a bad marriage, who sees herself as a victim—of her husband, of men in general, of the neighbors, of society—places a major burden on her daughter. Guilt seems to be involved in daughters' relationships with every variety of manipulative mother—but the Guilt-Monger uses it as an art form.

If your mother has been browbeaten into misery by her mother or her husband, it makes sense that she would look for relief from the one person over whom she has some control—her daughter. It makes sense for her—but not for you. She may be miserable, perhaps she truly has been victimized—but is it even possible for you to relieve the pain?

## The Healthy Adult: No Longer Her Mother's Responsibility

The adolescent girl gets through the painful realization that she is not going to win Dad away from Mom and learns to substitute new accomplishment for that fruitless goal. The healthy young woman is able to throw her energies into the development of her abilities, the growth of her creativity, the satisfaction gained from doing things well and making a difference. She moves into adulthood knowing that her parents do love her—though perhaps no longer the way she was loved as an infant. She is able to substitute new triumphs for old fantasies and find validation in the process.

She discovers that she can survive on her own, finds friends to support her, and meets men with whom she can experience new and different pleasures. She gets a job that not only gives her economic self-sufficiency, but enhances her self-esteem. She learns to enjoy her time alone and finds ways to express her inner being.

She is able to achieve independence and enjoy it, to succeed and feel good about it, to separate without feeling like she has been abandoned—or as if she has abandoned Mom. She is not overwhelmed with guilt.

## The Guilt-Monger's Daughter

More than any other reaction—more than rage, deprivation, or competition—daughters of difficult mothers talk about guilt. Mom does not have to be around to precipitate this most paralyzing and destructive legacy. It is there in your head all the time and you never know when the sirens will go off. When they do, guilt muffles all other emotions.

However, if you are ever to be your own person, you need to investigate why and when you feel this guilt, how it was instilled, and how you are clinging to it.

"When my mother cried," says Sharon, thirty-seven, "she never cried for me—she cried for herself. I went home once in the midst of a depression; I'd gained a lot of weight, felt awful about myself, wanted some comfort and care. We ended up having this terrible scene. To make matters worse, when I got back to my house, she called and said, 'I cried for weeks about what you looked like!'

"It was like that all through my childhood. She was orphaned at an early age and had been forced to work as a servant. I was brought up on these stories like they were fairy tales and would think, 'Look at this woman, look at how much more I have than she had at my age. Look at how much she is giving us.' When it was time to buy clothes, she would spend whatever it took to make sure we were well-dressed; yet there she was in her five-dollar housedress! There's something ironic about a mother spending exorbitant amounts on clothing for her kids, yet she looks like a cleaning lady. If I sound angry now it's because I never felt angry then. All I felt was guilty.

"I moved to Chicago but, for ten years, I was still living back with them in Wisconsin. When I would talk about home to my husband, I would mean Wisconsin. On Sunday afternoons, she would serve a big family meal and I wept every Sunday because I wasn't there. I thought about her constantly, worried about her. Every time she got sick, I felt guilty. Even when I was feeling good, she was on my mind.

"I remember once going to a party. I had two drinks and felt free and giddy. Under it all, I was thinking, 'If Mom were here, I wouldn't be doing this.' I always felt I was supposed to be home, taking care of her, and she never forgave me for going away to school. From that time on, she called me 'The Professor.' She always said, 'If you're not for me, you're against me,' and, by leaving, I had turned into the enemy.

"Last time I went home, I was a mess. I had gone on Prozac for my depression. I was so heavy I had developed heel spurs from the weight. My pain was so raw nobody could have missed it and I needed to reconnect with my family, my sisters. I had so looked forward to sharing a Sunday meal and good talk. My mother had slaved to do the food and what she wanted was for her efforts to be acknowledged, but my talking held up her schedule. She came in with the next course and we weren't done and she's at this emotional pitch to begin with so she starts calling me 'The Professor.' Things went from bad to worse.

"I'm thirty-seven years old and my mother is totally wiping me out, like she's always done, and I screamed, 'Why do you hate me so much?' I couldn't believe it was my voice; it was the sound of a wounded animal. All those years, I'd never thought my mother hated me but, that moment, that's the way I experienced it. My sisters and I started crying. My brother-in-law came and put his arm around me. My mother started yelling, 'Why are you doing this to me? Why are you telling me I'm a bad mother?'

"Unfortunately, about a year later, I had to go to them for money. I called to say that things were very serious. I was still depressed and on medication. I was trying to get better but I needed help.

"My mom flipped out. 'You're telling me this therapist is helping you? I've never seen you worse than when you were here. You can't walk, you're so heavy. You think this therapist is not getting something on the side from the psychiatrist who's prescribing the pills?' I thought I had heard it all but then she starts to weep, 'When you were here and you said those awful things to me, you were on drugs, weren't you?' That was when I realized that she was always going to be the victim and I was always to be the villain. And, of course, what she said hit home because, on some level, I do feel ashamed of taking an antidepressant and of how I had behaved. Guilt has a purpose. My mom uses it as a weapon."

## What's in Store for the Guilt-Monger's Daughter?

The daughter of the Guilt-Monger is locked into dependency because every move she makes toward adulthood reignites the guilt. She cannot enjoy her own accomplishments, sense her growing powers, or relish her independence, and thus the natural process of substituting achievement in the outside world for the support of the family cannot occur. The Guilt-Monger—who has sacrificed so much for her child—actually encourages her daughter to give up her identity as a woman and to remain a sexless child.

Perhaps the mother has been left by her husband and seems shattered by the trauma. The child is confused and upset by her mother's sighs and tears but, after the daughter has mourned the loss, she is ready to move forward. However, the daughter of the Guilt-Monger finds that she is always anxious because she is not at one with her depressed mother. If she visits her father, her mother makes her feel like she has consorted with the enemy.

The child thinks that she should be able to change what her mother feels. She transforms her confusion into the belief that it must have been her fault. There is more safety that way than in feeling totally helpless. "If it is my fault, I can change it. If only I hadn't been bad, it never would have happened."

> "I was afraid my mom would break like a piece of glass," says Cynthia, thirty-two. "I could never even cry as a child without the awareness that I was making her unhappy. Leaving home was out of the question because I owed it to my mother to take care of her. Even today, I feel wayward if I haven't called for two days. I have to visit even though she never asks me to come, never invites me over. There is simply the assumption of an obligation. I don't know what will make her happy so there is always the sense that I should be doing more. I'm forever taking her pulse, looking for her reaction."

This daughter makes herself feel less than whole because it is too threatening to acknowledge her own powers. She is afraid that she can hurt her mother. She worries that if she expresses anger, her mother will crumble.

> "Only recently," Cynthia continues, "did something new come into the picture, a tiny bit of perception, which is making me rethink everything. My mother was always a voracious reader. When I was a kid, she went through

one branch of the public library and started on another. Now she has lost the sight in one eye and the other is threatened. She has responded by saying if she can't read any more she doesn't want to live. 'I'm going to kill myself!' Is there anything worse a parent can say to a child?

"She'll threaten suicide but will she listen to books on tape? No way. She hires companions to read to her but then finds something wrong and fires them. The more she fires, the more I have to be there. I suddenly resolved that if she is going to make a weapon out of this blind- ness, I do not have to go along. I may feel sympathy— but I refuse to feel guilt."

If Cynthia gets free of her guilt, perhaps she can help her mother learn to accept her disability instead of wallow- ing in self-pity. A new mother–daughter relationship might be forged out of the transition. Guilt is a debilitating state that blocks growth. It buries anger, anxiety, envy, and fear—as well as boldness, courage, daring, and ingenuity. It suppresses anything Cynthia can do on her own behalf or any way of helping her mother. Only once she has gotten past the guilt can she understand the forces at play and start tackling the problems.

As the daughter of a Guilt-Monger, it may be possible for you to lead your mother toward some satisfaction in her life. Your independence may help her to find her own. By declaring your independence, you are not deserting her, nor are you forsaking your own needs. As you learn to connect with people differently, to make alliances that support you—you might be able to teach her to do the same. As you find a way to conquer your limitations, she might learn to conquer hers.

"For years after my father died, when my birthday came around, my mother would send me five dollars," says Alexis, now in her fifties. "She's on a limited income but she's not poverty-stricken. She could buy a scarf for seven. It's just terrible to get a five-dollar check, much worse than being forgotten. But what she was saying was, 'You have a man to buy you gifts and I don't,' and it made me more and more furious until, one year, I didn't even cash the check. Then her birthday would go by and I wouldn't send a card.

"Finally, I began to figure out that by getting so angry I was allowing the guilt entry. So, last year, I bought her a very nice gift and thought, 'She's going to have to get me one, too'—and she did! After suffering for years from those five-dollar gifts, I had gotten to a point where I was strong enough to turn things around. I said something to her about it being time we started to exchange nice gifts, that I really wanted to give her something nice this year. I said something mature and kind and it really did change things."

# Seeing Both Sides: A Mother-Daughter Workshop

Psychotherapist Leah Tolpin and her daughter, Ilana Tolpin Levitt, a career consultant and assistant dean for student affairs at Parsons School of Design, run mother–daughter workshops in New York City designed to open the door to communication, to educate the participants about women's development, to define the mother–daughter relationship. In the course of the workshop, participants learn to evaluate what is going on between them and to better understand what is causing any barriers. Both Tolpin and Levitt stress that the first step in the process is overcoming the shame and guilt.

"There is a lot of shame that the mothers messed up with the daughters," says Tolpin, "that one is not a good mother, one is not a good daughter."

"The daughter feels that she is not entitled to her own pain because the mother never complains," says Levitt. "When the daughter asks the mother how everything is, the answer is always 'Okay.' The daughter says, 'She's not suffering so I can't tell her about my suffering.' They protect each other by not sharing their pain. Guilt keeps them from communicating. The daughter wants to understand the mother. 'I am not fulfilling my life because you didn't fulfill yours,' she wants to say. Or 'You are living through me because you didn't fulfill your life and I feel guilty because I am not fulfilling mine.'"

The workshops start with the participants revealing why they came. "The daughters want the mothers to get their own lives," says Tolpin. "They want to know why the mothers are the way they are. They want them to stop focusing so much on them, or they haven't gotten enough from the mothers and are still angry and desperate to get what they didn't. They want their mothers to accept them for who they are and to stop judging them—and the mothers want a lot of the same things."

The participants do an exercise designed to reveal buried feelings.[1] The mothers and daughters are each asked to write down the animal, the texture, and the color that

---

1. For more information on these exercises, see Stephen J. Bergman and Janet Surrey, *The Woman–Man Relationship: Impasses and Possibilities* (Wellesley, Mass.: Stone Center, 1992).

best describes their relationship. They often come up with the same answers.

The most frequently named animal in the workshops is the cat; the cat needs love and wants to be petted but, the minute it wants freedom, it is aloof and gone. Women have named the koala bear or the kangaroo because of the protection, the pouch, the daughter feeling suffocated. Sometimes fierce animals like lions are named.

"For texture," says Tolpin, "one daughter who hadn't spoken to her mother in years came up with a bed of nails and the mother was hearing this."

"Corduroy comes up a lot," says Levitt, "because it is deep and smooth and has thick ridges. You can comfortably sink into the groove of it—but go the other way and it is coarse and doesn't make sense.

"The colors involve a lot of wishes. The mother is in denial and sees yellow and sunshine and the daughter sees red for her rage. 'That's the problem,' the daughter might say. 'You think things are so sunny and bright while I am furious!'"

The exercise allows the participants to talk about feelings and to get past the isolation and guilt by sharing in a group.

Then they split up: the mothers with Tolpin, the daughters with Levitt. They are asked to write down what they want to understand most about the other and what they want most for the other to understand about them.

"Some of the things the daughters want to understand," says Levitt, "are: Why is she so unassertive although she has great qualities? What does she want out of life for herself? Why is she disappointed and anxious so much of the time? Why did she marry my father? Why is she so needy? Why is she so controlling? Why can't she let go? Why didn't she become who she could have? Why can't she accept me for who I am? What is her pain?

"What they want their mothers to know is: 'I have my own life. I can make my own decisions. I have to take risks and fail but I will be okay.'

"Then we ask them what they want to stop doing, continue doing, start doing with their mothers. They want to continue spending time and sharing and communicating on an honest level. Instead of saying, 'Gotta go!' and hanging up the phone when they get irritated, they want to be able to say, 'You just pushed my buttons. I'm not comfortable talking to you about this.' They want respect and connection but they don't know how to get there because of the guilt and the anger. There is a shame about anger. 'How can you be angry with someone who has given your whole life to you?' they ask. Daughters cut off their mothers because they don't know how to separate any other way. They don't know how to balance spending time and giving something and still preserve themselves."

The final stage of the workshop is called negotiation— when the mothers and daughters tell each other what they wrote down and, with the support of the group, when they can say things that they have never said before. Others can help them articulate what they cannot say well.

Perhaps the mother says, "I care about you and something is on my mind and I need to say it." The daughter responds, "Say it in a way that I can hear it. If you blurt it out in the middle of something else, I can't." The three topics that most come up are separation, boundaries, and power.

## Separation

About separation, Tolpin says, "Anytime the daughter makes a choice that doesn't fit the mother's image, it is like a betrayal. It compromises the mother's identity. The daughters feel betrayed by the mothers and vice versa. The mothers feel they have given so much. The daughters feel obligated. The mothers feel abandoned. Then the guilt enters and the daughters feel they should be doing more, but they are really angry and feel imposed upon."

## Boundaries

"One mother stopped by with her friends to show off her grandchildren on a Sunday morning," Tolpin continues. "They were just driving by. The daughter was enraged. 'Don't just show up at my house,' she said. 'I have my own family.' The mother was terribly hurt. 'I'm proud of my grandchildren. I thought you'd be pleased.' The daughter said, 'Ask me like you would ask a friend. Don't make assumptions about what I feel.'"

"The mothers and daughters forget to adjust to an adult–adult relationship," adds Levitt. "It is still a mother–daughter relationship, but one with defined boundaries. Nobody can read another's mind, but the daughter is often afraid to establish boundaries because the mother will get so hurt. So, once again, guilt is an obstacle."

## Power

Often the mothers think they are suggesting something and the daughters feel it as a criticism. "The daughter gives the mother power that the mother doesn't realize she has," says Tolpin, "and the mother hears her own mother in her daughter's voice. So both feel intimidated and controlled."

"At the end," says Levitt, "When they share what they want, the mothers' and daughters' reactions are always similar. They both want to be understood for who they are. The mothers want to be accepted for their limitations and assets and for the daughters to understand their pain and where they've come from—and the daughters want the same."

"Working with mothers and daughters," Tolpin concludes, "we really see the pathos of the mothers and the struggles of the daughters. We see both sides."

# Separation: Reworking the Past

In her wrenching memoir, *Fierce Attachments,* feminist writer Vivian Gornick re-creates the love–hate relationship that kept her chained to her mother. Here she describes what her days were like when she was a little girl, living with her newly widowed mother:

> The air I breathed was soaked in her desperation . . .
> Her pain became my element, the country in which I
> lived . . . I longed endlessly to get away from her, but I
> could not leave the room when she was in it.[2]

When Gornick started working on the book, she intended to write a piece set entirely in the past about life with her mother as seen through her adolescent eyes. The writing seemed to be progressing as she got more and more involved in her memories, in her feelings, in the misery of that difficult time. Finally, she hit a paralyzing case of writer's block.

"Morning after morning," says Gornick, "I'd get up, stumble to my desk and stare at the blank page, let the hours pass, never get a word down. It was awful. The next day, I'd do the same. I couldn't let it go yet I could not move on. I didn't know what to do."

2. Vivian Gornick, *Fierce Attachments* (New York: Simon and Schuster, 1988), p. 77.

What was happening was that the past was overwhelming the present; she was sinking into her memories and her adult, competent, talented self was reverting to the helpless child she had been.

At the same time as she was going through this creative crisis, she was seeing her mother, now an old woman, once a week. However, her mother was no longer the weeping, shattered widow that Gornick remembered. Forty years had passed and the old woman was now a feisty survivor—a tough, loud, opinionated, fearless presence. She lived alone, had managed to build a successful life for herself, and had a great deal of pride in her independence. Indeed, there was a lot that was admirable about her that had nothing to do with Gornick's distant memories.

"Things were still touchy between us," says the writer, "as they had always been. But we had worked out a liveable truce. We saw each other once a week or so and took these long walks through the city. The streets were neutral turf. She couldn't criticize my apartment, I couldn't criticize hers. It helped keep the conversation impersonal and protected the boundaries between us. There was plenty to see and talk about on the streets so we could avoid the usual pitfalls. We both loved the city—and this helped us acknowledge the bonds between us. The walking was a pleasant way to handle the anxiety and provided good exercise. We had been doing it for years and it worked. More than that, on the walks I could even enjoy her. She ranted, she raved, she criticized passers-by, she judged everybody. Sometimes she said the most outlandish things. I had to laugh, was often shocked, couldn't believe her sensibility, her arrogance, her insight, her wit. This was not the mother

I remembered and sometimes I even liked her. Anyway, I used to think, 'I've got to write about these walks; I've got to use them.'

"Then, one day, when I was in the middle of this writing block, she did something so funny and astounding, I came home, sat down at the typewriter, and wrote exactly what had happened. Without judgement, without my opinions, not seeing her any more as a twelve year old but as a grown woman reporting on her mother. The words poured out and I knew at once that I had broken through and found my book."

In its final form, *Fierce Attachments* contains memories of Gornick's adolescent years with her widowed mother and the difficulties of her attempts to escape, balanced by clear-eyed vignettes of the two women in the present. The mother of the past is a powerful Guilt-Monger—a lost, miserable, selfish, clinging woman using her daughter for her own needs—and the daughter is a helpless accomplice who is afraid to leave her mother's side and move on into life.

In the sections dealing with the present, the mother is a funny, battling powerhouse. The daughter is a competent adult reporter with a flourishing career and, although many of the elements of the past still exist in their interactions, the reader is able to balance the internal perceptions of the child that was with the reality of the present. It is this contrast that makes the book an artistic success.

In addition, it was the writer's ability to drag herself out of the swamp of the past, to take a look at the present, to distance herself from her pain, and to temper her images of the all-powerful mother and the helpless daughter with a more accurate picture that enabled her to finish the book. What Gornick did in the process of creation was what we have been writing about all along—she managed to separate. And it freed her.

She could see where she had been a co-conspirator with her mother in the past—and where she was still behaving that way in the present. She could see the actuality of who she was in the present and who her mother was despite her internalized perceptions from her childhood. She was able to differentiate herself as a child from herself as an adult and her mother as she was from her mother as she is. She was able to see her mother in all her facets—both as a victim and as a survivor. She did not lose touch with her feelings, yet she gained objectivity. She saw and understood that if she was locked into a fierce attachment as an adult, it was as much her doing as her mother's. With these new insights, she was able to transform her energy into creative achievement.

Finishing the book, having it published to great acclaim, helped the separation process. Bit by bit, Gornick managed to struggle free of the past, of her anger and despair. We witnessed an extraordinary demonstration of that.

At a publication party for the paperback edition of Gornick's book, we found ourselves near the punch table with a white-haired woman, clearly in her eighties. We were amazed when she identified herself as Gornick's mother because this sweet, sparkling-eyed woman seemed far from the tough old cookie described in the book.

No question that it was she, however, because when we commented that she must be proud of her daughter, this little old lady hissed, in a stage whisper that sliced through the room, "I never went to college but if I coulda written it, it would have been a better book!"

Gornick clearly heard because her eyes flashed in impulsive anger. But, in a half second, her face relaxed. She shrugged as if to say, "I guess she'll never change!"

Then she smiled as everybody in the room raised a glass to toast her triumph.

# Strategies for Change

- Learn to move forward despite your guilt. Unlike other feelings, guilt cannot be released by expressing it. Communicating it does not bond you. Your mother may be pushing your buttons, but the wiring is in your brain. Battling its hold over you enables you to find out what you are truly feeling, frees you from the inner impasse, and makes your next encounter with your mother easier.
- Stop seeing your mother as a victim. When dealing with your mom, first acknowledge how much power she does wield. Then acknowledge how much power you possess. The Guilt-Monger is not going to dump you, no matter what you do. Other mothers (like the Critic) might never speak to you again if you challenge the status quo—but not the Guilt-Monger. If you do not believe this, test it out.
- Set up "guilt exercises" for yourself. Confront your guilt by acting despite it and see what happens. Consciously try to change your reactions. When your mother does something that usually sets you off, bite your tongue and do not take the bait. You will find that her power rests in your response. Once you refuse to go along with the guilt trip, you will feel freer.
- Be prepared for some anxiety and upset as you change. Consciously setting out to change your mother's behavior is not going to be comfortable for you. You might feel anxious and upset. If so, you will need to analyze what other emotions have been buried. But you can only get to that stage once your guilt has been spotlighted and disarmed.

- Strengthen the parts of your life over which you have control. Maintain a sense of your value separate from Mom by continuing to do things that you are good at. Give yourself time to accomplish your goals. Prepare for some setbacks and allow yourself to brush yourself off and try again. Make sure there is room in your life for introspection so that you can always keep a cool eye on what is going on, what has happened in the past, and why you are doing what you're doing.

- Set up a daily regimen for yourself: an exercise plan, a study course. This enables you to put the problem away for a moment and come back to it later. A change of environment is helpful, even taking a walk, because the past is pulling on you emotionally and it might be necessary to turn and look elsewhere. Find ways to relax: music, reading, sports. Exercise helps because you cannot obsess while fighting for deep breaths.

- Remember that your relationship with your mother is a part of your life; it is not your whole life. You are a competent wife, mother, career woman, and an adult. Your role as a daughter is not the only key to your identity. If you think her approval is going to wipe away your self-doubts, you will be disappointed. One's sense of self can never be so tied to anyone else's opinion.

# Conclusion:

# You As a Mother

Most of our readers, we presume, have identified with the daughter in the previous pages and stories. However, many of you have multiple roles. You are both daughters and mothers. You have a toddler or a teenager and you are concerned with whether you are passing problems on to your daughter, as your mother did to you.

Women who have struggled for their identity and independence, who were deprived of much of the nurturing and love they needed in childhood, and who are aware of these factors have the opportunity to become wise and loving mothers. They know about the losses, can share the pain, can feel for their offspring. They are the ones who can see what is going on, who can recognize what their child is going through—because they have been there themselves.

You can put all the pain and difficulty you have been through to good use. You can turn your suffering into wisdom. You can be a better mother to your daughter than your mother was to you, and you can heal some of your own wounds in the process.

Even if you never have children, you might have to assume the maternal role in your relationship with your aging mother. You too will be facing some of the problems we have outlined from both sides of the fence. This can make life more complex, but it can also offer new opportunities for development and growth.

As you care for your elderly mother and learn to forgive her, you can learn to be kinder to yourself. The reversal of roles reveals feelings never before expressed and can release both of you from grudging angers.

In the course of healthy mother–daughter relationships, one of the great advantages is that, as the daughter grows and changes, the mother can learn to grow and change, too. As the child passes through developmental stages, the parent can reexperience those stages herself. As the daughter overcomes her dependency on her mother, the mother is not necessarily left destitute. The healthy mother responds by moving on to the next phase in life, prodded by her daughter's courage, and the daughter is, in turn, inspired by the mother.

## Separation: A Difficult Task

Separation is not easy for most mothers. In our culture, particularly, the act of maternal bonding is romanticized and admired. Little girls practice nurturing and caring rituals with their dolls. Mothers who are always available, who perpetually offer their shoulders to cry on are idealized in film and on T.V.

But there is another component to motherhood that is just as important: mothers must learn how and when to let go of their children. Although this is often the core of father–son dramas on television, it is hardly ever mentioned as it pertains to young women.

Impulses in the child urge her to move on and away, but every step in the process of separation is two-fold for the mother. She is proud of her daughter as she grows into her own person—and yet she keenly feels a loss.

Good parenting requires you to be able to respond to the genuine emotions of your child, to reassure her that she will be loved as she gains independence, to convey a sense of soothing calm, which protects your daughter from feeling overwhelmed. Just as you learned how to nurture by practicing with your dolls, you need to learn how to let go—and very little training ground is available. There are no rituals for the separation process and few role models are available.

Let us conclude by taking what we have been investigating and applying it to the next generation. How can you, as a mother, make the mother–daughter relationship more encouraging of freedom and independence? How can you prevent crippling interactions from being passed from generation to generation?

## Strategies for a Healthy Relationship with Your Daughter

- Make sure that you listen to your daughter; give her and yourself time. When she comes to you with a problem, or even when she doesn't come (which might be more likely in certain stages), don't give in to your anxieties. Don't jump in and tell her what to do to resolve your tension. Don't assume you know what she is thinking or feeling. Separation requires space. Give her that as a gift.
- When she does come to you for help, remember that she needs to discover answers on her own. There are moments in life when she does not want you to solve her problems, no matter how needy she appears—although she still wants to share with you what is going on.

- Give your daughter some time to just "be." Every child needs some togetherness with you and some time alone in order to be in touch with her own inner workings. Try not to intrude on this essential process.

- Avoid overscheduling. Kids need to be able to walk along the street at their own pace. They need to step on cracks in the sidewalk and dawdle; they need to be able to stop and stare when something interests them. Try to establish some times when things are done according to your child's rhythms, when she can feel in charge, when she is not being hurried because you have chores to do, and when she does not feel the necessity to perform.

- Don't assume that she wants what you wanted. You may want to compensate for your past deprivations by offering her what you didn't get—but you may have a daughter who doesn't want that. What may be overstimulating to one child is good for another. We are all different. The sensitive parent tunes in to her child's unique personality.

- Don't take it personally when your daughter needs to hate you in order to grow. This is part of a natural developmental course. Try to be aware and respond to her internal state. When she yells "You never understand!" and slams out of the house, instead of responding by feeling hurt and fearful, recognize that it comes from her need to separate.

- Establish priorities and allow her some control. For example, you cannot allow a three year old to cross the street on her own, but if she wants to wear the same outfit every day, let her. You cannot allow a teenager to drink and drive, but if she wants to paint her room purple, let her.

- As she grows, support her in the separating process. Be aware of how helpful peer relationships are to her in this. When she wants to talk for hours on the phone to her best friend, remember this is part of her move into independence. When she keeps secrets, starts a diary—as tempted as you may be—don't pry.

- Encourage her to form other attachments. If she raves about a scout leader and you find yourself envious and competitive, try not to put the scout leader down. She can be a bridge in the separation process and is not going to replace you as a mother.
- Allow her to see you as only human. When she is old enough and can handle the information, be aware when you make mistakes with her and talk about them openly. In this way, you let her know that you are human, not an ideal, and have no need to deny reality when she catches you in an overreaction or an anxious moment.
- Recognize how intense and important the mother–daughter bond is. Your daughter is not going to abandon you. She is not going to forget you. An honest mother–daughter relationship is one of the great joys of a woman's life and it is worth the struggle for both parties.

## Achieving Emotional Health

Emotional health and maturity are not fixed states. You are not anointed as healthy at a particular moment in life and without fear forever after. A marriage doesn't make you emotionally healthy. A brilliant therapist can't do it. It doesn't come in a flash from the skies. Emotional health is an ongoing experience and backsliding always threatens. A crisis occurs and your childhood fears blossom and you have to struggle to master them once again.

You did it as an infant, as an adolescent, as a young adult. You renegotiate the same territory over and over. Many assumptions about your abilities have been learned, but, as ingrained as these might be, what was learned can be changed. The more you decide that you will not allow some childhood limit to keep you from adult satisfaction, the more prepared you are to overcome obstacles. But the struggle never ends. As soon as you reach one level of maturity, you have to deal with the next. Separation from a parent comes in stages. There is no finish line. The important thing is to never stop reaching.

Our aim in life is to keep growing, to keep changing, to constantly discover new facets of ourselves, and to develop new abilities as life demands them. The greatest harm we can do to ourselves is to allow our fears to lock us into a stage of development so that we cannot move forward. Emotional maturity is not the achievement of "happiness"; it is not feeling released and relieved of all fears and worries. We aim for the attainment of freedom of choice so that we can respond to the real needs of our lives with new growth—instead of being tossed back to the past.

As much as separation is healthy, so is the ability to bond. The ability to be intimate, to trust, to love are essential if one's life is to be rich and full. These are learned from our parents, particularly from our mothers. The desire to be separate from her is as important as the desire to stay close to her. Our health is in the balance of the two.

Clearly, it is a positive thing if you love your mother and if you have a close and intimate friendship with her. This is wonderful for you and for her; this is wonderful for your daughters. However, as we've discussed, with some mothers this sort of intimate friendship is not possible. In these cases, it is important to salvage whatever you can. It is important to work with what you've got, to create a relationship and maintain it—one that allows your mother to stay in your life without overwhelming it, that allows you to see her and deal with her while you both maintain some individual control over your lives.

We are not saying that you must cut your invasive mother out of your life completely in order to live successfully. We are not even saying that she is the core of all your problems.

You're an adult now and her inadequacies, her failures no longer have the power to harm you. You also have the power to behave differently with your own daughters—or with your mother as she ages—and, in that change, new horizons open for you, new possibilities for healing develop, and bright, new joys await you in life.